Called by God

Stories from the Jewish and Christian Bibles

Alan Robinson

THE *Alpha* PRESS

BRIGHTON • PORTLAND

Copyright © Alan Robinson 2002

The right of Alan Robinson to be identified as author of this work has been asserted in accordance with the Copyright, Designs and Patents Act 1988.

2 4 6 8 10 9 7 5 3 1

First published *2002, in Great Britain by*
THE ALPHA PRESS
PO Box 2950
Brighton BN2 5SP

and in the United States of America by
THE ALPHA PRESS
5824 N.E. Hassalo St.
Portland, Oregon 97213–3644

British Library Cataloguing in Publication Data
A CIP catalogue record for this book is available from the British Library.

Library of Congress Cataloging-in-Publication Data
Robinson, Alan.
Called by God : stories from the Jewish and Christian Bibles.
p. cm.
ISBN 1-898595-40-2 (alk. paper)
1. Bible O.T.—Biography. 2. Bible stories, English—O.T.
I. Title.
BS571.R44 2002
221.9'22—dc21
2002010127

Cover illustration: Daniel in the Lions' Den, from Bordj El Loudi, Roman, 5th century (mosaic)/Bridgeman Art Library.

Typeset and designed by G&G Editorial, Brighton
Printed by TJ International, Padstow, Cornwall
This book is printed on acid-free paper.

CALLED BY GOD

CONTENTS

{ v }

CONTENTS

PREFACE

This book is intended as an introduction to the principal characters in the first part of the Christian Bible (Old Testament) and, of course, in the Jewish Bible. After exploring these pages, the reader may then wish to read the original material. The stories presented are not meant in any way to replace the stories in the Bible, for this of course would be impossible. At the same time, it is unfortunately true that some Christian or Jewish people do not read these stories and prophecies very frequently. Certainly it is not easy to read, for example, the Book of Job, or the whole of Ezekiel's writings. If, however, the summaries of these two sections as presented in the following pages are read in the few minutes it would take, then the reader may more readily understand the general message of these and other biblical books. Thus a prime purpose of the book is to enable the reader to go back to the originals with more confidence.

The author has endeavoured to write the stories in a simple, though dignified style, fitting for the interpretation of sacred scriptures. The reader must make a personal judgement as to whether this objective has been achieved. The first three sections, which tell the stories of the patriarchs Abraham, Isaac and Jacob, have been written in a slightly more relaxed style than the other sections, because this seems appropriate for these narratives.

Each of the characters included in the book was convinced of a divine calling. His or her experiences were recorded either by the character personally or by a disciple or a later editor. Scholars have been delving into the original material for centuries and various conclusions have been reached. For example, some people believe Abraham was a historical person and others do not. Some people believe that the writings of Amos are original to him, while others do not. The issues revolving round these various interpretations are a fascinating study. Abraham, for example, might have lived around 1750 BC, whereas the Book of Daniel might have been produced in the 2nd century BC. Thus the scriptural books cover over fifteen hundred years of history and editorial activity by their authors. Even though the people described in the book are very different, the important quality they have in common is a belief in a supreme God who revealed himself to them. They were *chosen by God*.

My book is offered as an attempt to make God's word more comprehensible to believers, as well as to introduce people to some fascinating records of the past, which are revered by the adherents of two of the world's major religions. There is also a connection with Islam because some of the characters described also appear in the Qur'an. (Items starred on the contents page indicate a Quranic connection.)

ABRAHAM
FATHER OF MANY NATIONS

I

ABRAM looked into the sun flickered stream,
thinking of Ur and wondering how long the water flow
would take to reach the city of his birth.
It had been slow journeying up the narrowing Euphrates,
but Terah had led them well,
and neither man nor beast had missed the way.
Yet Abram knew the time had come to separate:
he and his father must now follow different paths –
the God Almighty had decreed it should be so.
Still, he was sad, for Terah was his father after all,
and all the tribes were strong, bound by ties of blood.
Abram walked back to the tents, pitched outside Haran,
and went to tell his wife of God's new plan;
and then with heavy heart he sought his father
to break the news. And so it came about
that Abram and his nephew Lot set off
to the south country where the pastures were
lush green, at least according to the market chat.
The tents were packed, the donkeys loaded
and the clan walked towards the midday sun,
the women gossiping along
and coltish children playing hide and seek among the rocks.
The men were armed, and watched the flocks and herds
with care, wary of rustlers, bears and thieving lions,
leaving their talk till evening time
when fragrant pots were simmering on the fires.

As he marched sturdily through patient days
Abram thought long on what the Lord had promised.
Could it be true, that he, now leader of a tiny clan,
would one day be more famous than his father,
would be well known throughout the world?
Sometimes he doubted what God's Spirit seemed to say,
but then, he thought again of how he had been called,

so clearly listening to the heavenly voice.
It must be true. It must be so.
But only time would tell.

The clan arrived in Canaan and they all rejoiced,
for the rich valleys were good for cattle
and the hills for sheep.
Abram decreed that all should pray
beside the altar that he raised beside a mighty oak,
at Moreh near to Shechem.
And there he had another vision, while alone
on a bare hillside, and the Lord revealed
that the whole land would be a home
for his descendants for all time.

The clan marched on, until they came
to Bethel, House of God,
and nearby they pitched their tents.
Abram prayed there, but the Spirit ordered him
to journey further south
into the loneliness of the Negeb
where stony ridges pondered endlessly
under vast, cloudless skies.

II

ABRAM AND LOT both prospered
and their flocks and herds abounded in the land,
and both were blessed with gold and silver.
Their wives were sleek and richly jewelled,
their children plump and strong.
But grazing was scarce for so many beasts
and Abram knew that he and Lot would have to part;
he graciously allowed his nephew choice of land,
and Lot selected the palm groves and verdant slopes
along the Jordan valley, camping near to Sodom.

Now Sodom had a reputation for its people's wickedness,
but Lot was happy in his choice,

for he became the richest man around that place,
and men saluted him with great respect –
for his vast wealth.

Abram stayed in Canaan happily enough,
for now the grazing was less scarce.
From time to time he moved his tents
and at Hebron built an altar for his clan
that they might worship faithfully
the God who spoke so plainly to their leader.

Morning and evening Abram prayed,
going aside to be alone
with the miracles of dawn and dusk.
One morning Abram stood upon a hill
and watched the sun reveal the glory of the landscape,
far rolling hills, eye stretching to blue distances.
Within he heard the voice of God:
look to the west, and to the east;
look to the south and to the north –
this land is all for you and those who will come after you,
so wander where you will, and I shall be with you,
day upon day, night upon night,
and I will give you my protection and my blessing.
Abram gave thanks to his Almighty God
and roamed the hills and valleys with his growing clan.
His one regret, which seeded doubt about God's promise,
was his own childlessness.

III

KINGS from the wilderness rode with loud thunder
into the valley around the Salt Sea;
rich booty and prisoners they captured,
then left for their homes with heart dancing glee.
News came to Abram that Lot had been taken,
and men from his tribe gathered in force;
they galloped away southwards and fought a great battle,
defeating the legions of many great kings.

Lot was soon rescued and Abram returned,
thankful that God had given him success.
He went to the city of Salem to pray
and met the high priest at the wide open gates.
Melchizedek was king there by God's gracious will,
and welcomed his gallant, victorious ally.
The great king of righteousness brought out some bread
and flasks of red wine to render thanksgiving.
He prayed for God's blessing on Abram that day
and Abram presented the king with his tithe.
Sodom's wild king offered to Abram
the spoils of the battle, but Abram refused any gift,
to preserve his good name and his vow to the Lord,
to whom he was bound for a life time of service.

IV

ABRAM prayed long that children would be his,
but Sarai was not blessed;
so Abram called his servant Eliezer
and made him heir to all he had.
But still the Lord vowed that an heir
would spring to life from Abram's fathering.
God's promise was renewed and he revealed
that countless children would be born in Abram's line
and that they would own the land farther than eye could see
or mind conceive.
Abram laid out a sacrifice to God, and then he slept
deeply and long as dusk descended all around.
And Abram dreamed a burning torch and smoke and fire
were drawn across the sacrifice that he had made.
When he awoke, he knew the Lord had spoken yet again;
he knew the promise would be kept in God's good time.
He said, *God's covenant is sure and I shall be*
the father of a tribe who will be dedicated
to God's work in this land,
and this strange vision is a sign for me.

V

STILL, Sarai had no child,
but Abram joined with Hagar, Sarai's servant,
and soon she bore a son and Ishmael was his name.
Hagar was proud, and Sarai was humiliated
and treated Hagar cruelly.
So into desert ways the girl ran off,
taking Ishmael with her and weeping as she went.
But angels guarded her and told her that her son
would be the father of a desert race.
Hagar gave thanks to God All Seeing
and then returned to Abram's camp,
willing to serve her mistress humbly day by day,
for now she knew that God was with her.

VI

ABRAM was old, and still no child by Sarai,
but he lived close to God and prayed
that God would walk with him,
to guide him in his every deed,
to pour abundant grace like oil upon his head.
And God renewed his promise of descendants
scattered across the earth, and said,
Your name will now be Abraham,
great father of a multitude of nations;
and Sarai's name from now is changed to Sarah,
a princess famed and honoured .for all time.
Abraham then at God's command
was circumcised and ordered Ishmael and the other men
to mark themselves with this new sign of covenant.

VII

ABRAHAM'S tent was by a shady oak,
and often he relaxed at noon,
shielded from scorching sun, as he thought long

of God's abundant promises.
One day three travellers passed by,
and Abraham rose up to welcome them;
he brought them drinks and washed their feet
while Sarah cooked some bread and meat.
And while the men were dining there,
in the cool shade of the oak,
Abraham stood by to meet their every need.
The men seemed strange,
and different from the usual passers by –
there was an air of mystery
about their presence, almost as if three angels
had wandered down from heaven.
After a while, one visitor enquired where Sarah was,
and Abraham replied that she was in the tent.
The man went on, *In spring we shall return,*
and Sarah will undoubtedly bring forth a son.
But Sarah heard and laughed at this vain hope,
for she was old and past the age of giving birth.
Why is your wife amused? the angel said.
The Lord has power over all that is,
and surely he can breathe a child to life.
Sarah came out and said she had not laughed,
but then the angel's face grew stern:
Indeed you did! Yet even so the Lord will bless your womb.

VIII

THE CITIES in the valley were infamous for sin,
but Lot had settled there, in Sodom, where
his house was well appointed,
and his daughters found themselves rich men to marry,
and life seemed good to Lot and all his family.
But Abraham was told that God would soon destroy
both Sodom and Gomorrah.
He prayed that God would change his mind –
if any righteous men were found within the cities.
But the hour came when God decreed
that earthquake, fire and brimstone should obliterate

the cities of the valley and all the people there.
Just before calamity descended on the towns
some messengers arrived to warn the family of Lot
to leave immediately and never to return.
The angels guided Lot, his wife, and both their daughters
to a place of safety, and told them not to stop
and not to look behind.
But Lot's wife turned to look back at the city,
and while she stood disaster overtook her,
petrifying her to salt, a lonely pillar in the wilderness.
Lot was reduced to dwelling in a cave, his daughters with him.

IX

ISAAC was born to Sarah, and she was filled
with joy and laughter at this gift from God:
the boy was circumcised
to show that he was bearer of God's covenant.
Later, a celebration for the weaning of the boy was held
and Abraham was proud to have a son so handsome.
But Sarah's heart was filled with jealousy
when at the feast she saw Ishmael playing with Isaac,
for she hated Hagar who had borne a child before her.
And Sarah said that Hagar and her son should go,
but Abraham was fond of Ishmael
and wanted them to stay.
But by God's will Hagar and Ishmael left,
though with God's promise
that the boy would be the father of a nation.
Abraham provided food and water
and mother and child were driven to the wilderness.
Hagar was devastated at her banishment
and feared for the life of Ishmael;
but God heard Ishmael's cries and Hagar's prayers
and led her to a well of water,
promising again that Ishmael would be great
and blessed with progeny.
Ishmael grew strong and skilled with bow,
caring for Hagar lovingly.

She found a wife for him and happiness
surrounded them amidst their growing family.

X

ABRAHAM was sorely tested by his God,
for he was told to sacrifice his son,
his much loved son whom Sarah bore to him.
He saddled up his ass, and travelled with the boy
into the mountains of Moriah, two servants with them.
Near to the chosen place, they cut some wood
and Abraham and Isaac climbed the hill,
with the wood loaded onto Isaac's shoulder.
Isaac was puzzled when they reached their destination,
and so he said, *My father, we have the wood, we have the fire,
but here there is no lamb to sacrifice.*
And Abraham declared, *The sacrifice will be provided
by God himself, my son.*
So Abraham erected there an altar, and upon it laid the wood,
ready to burn the sacrifice; and then he tied his son
and laid him gently on the stack of wood.
He took his knife and was about to strike his son,
but the Lord called to him, *Abraham, Abraham!*
And Abraham replied, *Lord, I am here.*
The voice went on, *Do not harm the boy,
for now I know that you are faithful and obedient,
and you have not withheld your son from me.*
Then Abraham observed a ram, trapped in some thorns,
and offered up the animal in sacrifice to God.
He thanked the Lord for all his providential care;
and God renewed his promise of a blessing
upon the family of Abraham in future years.

XI

AFTER the death of Sarah, Abraham decided
that Isaac should be married to a kinswoman
from the land that he had left at God's command.

He sent his servant there to find a wife for Isaac,
and when the servant reached the city,
he took his camels to the well to water them.
He asked the Lord to guide him in his choice,
and Rebekah came to draw some water;
it was she who fulfilled the sought for sign
by offering to water all the servant's camels.
The servant gave her a ring and golden bangles
when he had ascertained that she
was cousin to the family of Abraham;
and then he asked her if her father would allow him
to stay the night under his roof.
Rebekah's brother Laban came to the well
to ask the servant over to his house to have a meal;
and then and there the servant told his tale,
revealing the relationship between the family
of Abraham and that of Laban and Rebekah.
Then it was agreed a marriage should take place
between Rebekah and the son of Abraham;
the servant poured out gifts for all the family,
and then they left for Canaan, where Isaac waited for his bride.
Isaac was in the fields when first Rebekah came,
thinking of his God and the mystery of the future;
after the servant had recounted all his doings,
Rebekah and Isaac came together
and love grew between them in the Lord.

XII

ABRAHAM took to himself another wife
whose name was Keturah;
she bore him several sons,
but all his wealth he was to leave to Isaac,
though to his other sons he gave generously,
then sent them east to live elsewhere.
At last, he harvested his many years
and his two oldest sons, Isaac and Ishmael,
buried their father in the family cave.
The Lord had promised that Abraham

would father many people, and so it was:
thousands of years beyond his grave
his name would be renowned throughout the earth.

ISAAC
BEARER OF THE CONVENANT

I

NOW ISAAC AND REBEKAH lived and loved
for many years, but sadly had no child;
so Isaac prayed that God would bring a child to them,
and soon Rebekah felt the kick of twins within her womb.
She prayed for guidance from the Lord,
and this was God's response:
Two nations struggle in your womb
and they shall be at enmity,
and one shall be the stronger,
but even so, the older will attend the younger.
And when the twins were born,
the first was hairy, rough and red,
and he was named as Esau.
And the second boy was named as Jacob,
and he was quiet and smooth skinned.

II

THE TWINS grew up, blessed with good health,
but Esau was an outdoor man who loved to hunt,
while Jacob liked to stay at home around the tents.
Esau was loved by Isaac, for his father enjoyed the game
that Esau brought from hunting expeditions;
but Jacob pleased his mother and she gave him all her love.
One day Esau came home, tired and ravenous.
Smelling the meal that Jacob was then cooking,
Esau asked his brother for a dish of stew.
But Jacob had in mind the birthright of his brother,
and would not give to Esau what he craved,

unless he swore to sell his birthright to his younger brother.
Esau agreed, and Jacob fed him well;
and so it was that Esau gave away his future blessing
for a bowl of soup and a few chunks of bread.

III

FOR SOME TIME, Isaac went to live in Gerar,
where he pretended that Rebekah was his sister.
This was to thwart those rogues
who might assassinate a man to steal his lovely wife.
But Abimelech saw him with Rebekah
and realised that she must be his wife,
and Isaac then explained his ploy,
at which Abimelech offered his protection.
As time went on, Isaac became the envy of his neighbours,
for he was rich and owned vast flocks and herds;
and Abimelech saw the wealth of Isaac,
and being envious, invited him to leave.
In the broad valley that he found,
Isaac constructed wells, but these caused further strife
with other herdsmen in that place.
So Isaac took his flocks to Beersheba
where the Lord appeared to him in a night vision,
saying, *I am the God of Abraham your father;*
you must not be afraid, for I am with you,
and I will bless you, and your descendants after you.
There Isaac raised an altar to the Lord,
and worshipped reverently with all his tribe.
From that day on he lived in peace
and covenanted with his neighbours.

IV

WHEN ISAAC was old and nearly blind, he sent for Esau,
and asked his son to go out hunting for some game.
And Isaac said, *I wish to eat a tasty meal before I die:*
when you bring this about, my blessing will be yours.

⟨ 11 ⟩

Rebekah heard this conversation
and she sent for Jacob so that she could warn him
of his father's last intent. She said to Jacob,
If you bring me two kids I shall prepare a meal,
and you can take it to your father,
and you will then receive his blessing.
But Jacob said, *My father will know by touch that I am Jacob,*
for Esau is hairy and I am smooth.
His mother charged her son to do what she had said,
and then she made a hearty meal for Isaac.
She gave to Jacob Esau's clothes
and placed upon his hands skin from the kids.
So Jacob took the meal to Isaac
who was convinced that Jacob was his other son.
The old man was surprised that Esau had returned so quickly,
but Jacob lied and said, *The Lord was with me, father.*
Then Isaac drew his son nearer to him and said,
You sound like Jacob, lad,
but hairy hands like these belong to Esau.
To make sure Isaac smelled the clothes that Jacob wore,
and then, completely convinced, he gave the younger twin
the blessing due to Esau.
It was a powerful blessing – Isaac's last will and testament,
and it was irreversible.
But almost right away, Esau came in, wanting a blessing
from his father, who trembled at the thought
of how the blessing had been wrongly given.
Esau then pleaded with his father, bitterly complaining
that Jacob had robbed him of his birthright.
To that request his father gave a firm refusal:
Your brother has my blessing now,
and you shall serve him as your master;
by sword and violence you shall live,
but from your brother you will at some time free yourself.
Esau decided that he would despatch his brother,
but when Rebekah heard about his plot,
she forewarned Jacob of his brother's purpose.
She advised Jacob to go to stay with Laban,
his uncle in Haran, and said that she would send for him
when Esau's fury had abated.

Before Jacob departed, his father blessed him once again,
advising him to marry one of Laban's daughters.
Esau decided he would marry also,
and took to wife a daughter of his kinsman Ishmael.

JACOB
WHOSE NAME IS ISRAEL

I

As JACOB travelled to Haran
he sometimes slept under the stars;
on one such night he took a stone to be his pillow
and there he fell asleep.
Now while he slept he dreamed, and saw a ladder
stretching from earth to heaven;
and hosts of angels went both up and down the ladder,
while God himself stood high above.
And God spoke to Jacob, saying,
I am the Lord of heaven and earth;
I am the God of Abraham your forefather;
I am the God of Isaac;
I give to you and your descendants all this land
that lies around you;
your countless seeds shall be scattered
to north and south and east and west;
all families across the world will bless your name;
I shall be with you wheresoever you go
and to this land you shall return.
Jacob awoke from sleep and was afraid.
He thought, *God must be here,*
in this truly awesome place,
and this must be the very house of God
whose gateway leads to heaven above.
He took the stone on which his head had lain,
anointing it with oil, and then he raised it
as a pillar of remembrance to the house of God,
and so he named that place as Bethel.
He vowed that he would serve his Lord

his whole life through, from that day on,
relying on the providence of God
and giving Him a tenth of all his goods.

III

JACOB approached Haran
and met some shepherds by a well
waiting to water their sheep.
He asked them if they knew his uncle,
Laban of Haran, and they said they did.
One of the shepherds said, *Look over there,*
Rachel his daughter is shepherding her father's sheep.
Rachel approached the well
and Jacob rolled away the stone that topped the well
that she might water all her sheep.
And then he told her that he was her cousin,
and they kissed, and overcome, they wept.
She ran to tell Laban that Rebekah's son had come to visit;
his uncle greeted him with warmth
and made him welcome there.

III

LABAN AND JACOB agreed that Jacob should be paid
for any work he did while staying in Haran.
When asked how much he thought his pay should be,
Jacob suggested that Rachel and he should marry
as part of the agreement.
Laban agreed but said that Jacob should delay
the marriage for seven years at least.
Jacob was happy there, as years flew by,
and when the seven years had passed
he asked for Rachel's hand in marriage.
To celebrate the wedding, Laban gathered all his men
and gave a feast for everybody in his care.
That evening Jacob went to meet his wife and slept with her,
but when morning arrived he found that he had slept with Leah,

the older daughter, who was not as beautiful as Rachel.
Jacob went to see his uncle and he said to him,
You have deceived me, Laban –
why have you tricked me in this way?
Laban replied, *Surely it is the custom*
for the older daughter to be married first.
But if you work another seven years
my daughter Rachel will be yours.
And so it came about, after this time had passed,
that Jacob married Rachel also.
Unhappily for Leah,
Jacob loved the younger sister more.

IV

THE LORD had pity upon Leah and rewarded her
by giving her a son whose name was Reuben;
successively she bore three other sons,
whose names were Simeon and Levi and Judah.
Rachel was envious because she bore no children,
and she remonstrated with her husband Jacob,
but he said plainly, *God has shut your womb, not I.*
Now Rachel had a maid whose name was Bilhah
and she decreed that she could be a wife to Jacob;
and from this union
Bilhah bore a son whose name was Dan,
and then another son whose name was Naphtali.
Now Leah, worried that she might have no more children,
gave her maid Zilpah as a wife for Jacob,
and she had two sons whose names were Gad and Asher.
Now Leah had some potent fruits that Reuben found
and Rachel asked for some, but Leah was unwilling,
until Rachel promised her
that Jacob would be hers that night.
And so it came about that Leah bore another son,
whose name was Naphtali; and yet again she bore a son
and she named him Issachar.
Leah was joyful at her fruitfulness,
but Rachel's womb was closed

until the Lord had mercy on her plight.
So at last Rachel bore a son
whom she called Joseph;
and then she prayed also for yet another son
to bless her womanhood.

V

JACOB decided that the time had come
to journey home to his own country,
but Laban asked him if he would remain
and asked what wages Jacob would require.
So Jacob asked if he could have
any lambs or goats with speckled fleece
and all black lambs born in the flocks.
Laban agreed, but secretly removed the beasts so marked
and sent them on a three day journey with his sons.
But as time went on, many speckled lambs and goats were born,
and black lambs regularly appeared;
so Jacob separated them and became very rich,
while Laban's flocks grew weak and feeble.
Laban and Jacob disagreed and all the sons of Laban
were twisted with their jealousy of Jacob;
but God spoke to Jacob:
Go home to your own land, to the rich land of your fathers,
and I will journey with you, and I will guard your ways.
Rachel and Leah agreed to go with him,
for they were not respected by their family.

VI

JACOB prepared his family and flocks and herds
for their long journey down to Canaan;
his sons and wives were riding camels,
while hired men drove the animals along.
Before they left, Rachel had stolen from her father
the household gods which were his prize possession,
though Jacob did not know that she had done so.

The fugitives were far away beyond the wide Euphrates
before the Aramean, Laban, realised his loss.
Jacob reached Gilead, with Laban following hard;
and God revealed to Laban in a vision
that he should not speak harm or hurt to Jacob.
The two men met
and Laban asked why Jacob had deceived him,
maintaining that he would have let his nephew go
with happiness and joyful song.
But Jacob said that he had been afraid.
Then Laban charged Jacob with stealing all the household goods,
which Jacob honestly denied.
There was a search of tents and saddle bags,
but Rachel sat upon her camel, the goods under her legs;
and she complained that she could not come down
because she was not well.
Laban and Jacob quarrelled with some heat
but finally they made a covenant of friendship,
raising a pillar of stone to mark their new agreement;
and there they ate a meal together,
and Laban went back home.

VII

JACOB sent word to Esau of his return to Canaan,
telling him of his family news;
and Esau sent word back to say
that he would meet with Jacob;
but Jacob's messenger reported that his brother
would arrive accompanied by several hundred men.
Jacob was worried by this and so divided flock and herd
in two, each group travelling separately,
in case his brother stole his sheep and goats and cattle.
Then Jacob prayed that God would save him
from attacks by Esau, and reminded God
of what He had once promised.
So he set out to meet his brother, bearing many gifts
of camels, rams and asses, and of bulls and cows.
The servants were instructed to keep the droves apart,

and to present them one by one to Esau
as presents from his long lost brother.
And so it was that Jacob hoped to make his peace with Esau.

VIII

ON HIS WAY, Jacob brought his wives and servants
and all eleven sons to cross the River Jabbok;
and Jacob spent the night alone.
He wrestled with a man throughout the night
fighting with him until the rising of the sun.
Jacob would not give in, so the man
put Jacob's thigh out of joint
by pressing on the hollow of his thigh.
At last, Jacob's opponent said,
Let me go now, for dawn is breaking on the hill.
But Jacob said, *Before I let you go
you must extend to me your blessing.*
The man then said, *What is your name?*
When Jacob said his name, the man went on,
*From now your name is Israel,
because you have prevailed against both God and man.*
Jacob then asked the man how he was called,
and the man said, *Why do you ask my name?*
and blessing Jacob, went away.
Jacob was awed by this encounter,
knowing he had seen the face of God,
yet had survived to tell the tale.
And that is why he named that place Peniel –
the face of God.

IX

AS JACOB and his company went forward,
Jacob saw Esau and his fighting men approaching,
so he arranged in order
his wives and maids and all their children,
while he himself stood at the front.

When Esau drew up
Jacob bowed down before his brother seven times
and Esau ran to meet him.
Esau embraced him and they both wept,
their parting long ago recalled;
and Jacob introduced his children
and all their mothers, and all bowed down.
Then Esau said, *Why have you sent me so many gifts?*
Jacob replied, *To find your favour, Esau, my lord.*
Reluctantly Esau accepted Jacob's gifts
and Jacob praised his brother warmly,
saying, *Your face is like the face of God to me*
and you are gracious to your brother.
Esau suggested they should accompany each other
along the road, but Jacob declined,
so Esau said, *Well, let a party of my men*
go with you and all your flocks and herds
to guard you from all troubles.
Jacob again refused the offer of his brother
and made his way to Shechem
and there he bought a plot of land
where he could make his camp,
and reverently he raised an altar to the Lord.

X

Now DINAH, daughter of Leah
was loved by Jacob and her brothers;
she was a comely girl and soon a man called Shechem
decided that he loved her, but he seized her
and forced her into bed with him.
He wished to marry Dinah and his father gave approval;
but Jacob heard his daughter had been forced
and told his sons about the seizure of their sister.
The brothers were enraged and made a plan
to take revenge in honour of their sister;
and so when Shechem's father made advances,
offering hospitality and trade,
they readily agreed, but on condition

that Shechem's tribe should all be circumcised.
Both Shechem and his father
were in favour of this form of covenant,
and all their men agreed to do their part.
When three days had elapsed, two sons of Jacob,
Levi and Simeon, massacred the men of Shechem
and plundered all their goods.
Jacob their father was displeased, for he could see
that now their position in that area
was very much at risk;
but the two brothers were at ease
with how they had behaved
in seeking their revenge for Dinah's violation.

XI

AT GOD'S CALL Jacob returned to Bethel
and the whole tribe gave up their alien gods;
the Lord protected them as they passed by
cities and towns which held potential danger.
At Bethel God renewed his promise that
Jacob's descendants would be multiplied
and that great kings would spring forth in his line,
to rule the land that was within God's gift.
Rachel was then with child again and she
gave birth to Benjamin, but Rachel died
and Jacob mourned his loss by raising up
a tomb upon her grave, a lasting monument.
So Jacob had now fathered twelve strong sons
and each one bore a mighty tribe of Israel

JOSEPH
THE DREAMER

I

JOSEPH was shepherd to his father's flocks
and was the most loved son in Jacob's eyes.

Now Joseph wore a precious robe, a gift
from Jacob, and the other sons were jealous
of Joseph's preference in their father's heart.
At times, Jacob had dreams and one of these
pictured his brothers and himself at work
binding corn sheaves, and the brothers' sheaves bowed
towards the sheaf of Joseph. When he told
his brothers of his dream their envy grew,
and they refused to think of him as chief
among them. Then he had another dream
in which he saw the sun and moon bow down,
and stars, eleven all told. Jacob rebuked
his son and said, *Surely you do not think*
that I, your mother, and your brothers will
bow down to you. But Jacob strangely knew
his son would one day be a man of power.

II

THE BROTHERS went to mind their father's flocks
while Joseph stayed at home; but Jacob wished
to know how things were going, and so he sent
Joseph to see, instructing him to bring
what news there was about his other sons.
After enquiries, Joseph found his brothers,
and they conspired to kill him out of spite.
But Reuben would not let Joseph be killed.
He said, *Throw him into this pit and leave*
him there, but shed no blood. Reuben designed
to come back later, so that he might take
Joseph back home to be with his fond father.
But while they ate, a caravan went by,
some Ishmaelites with camels bearing gum,
and balm and myrrh to trade in Egypt's markets.
Joseph was sold to them for twenty shekels
and he was taken into Egypt as a slave.
The brothers covered Joseph's coat with blood
and took it to their father, who at once
knew it was Joseph's. Weeping, Jacob said,

Joseph has been devoured by a beast
of prey. And Jacob would not be consoled.

III

JOSEPH was sold to Potiphar, a captain,
a favoured officer in Pharaoh's guard;
Joseph did well and soon had charge of all
the household, which was richly blessed by God.
Now Joseph was a handsome man and soon
the wife of Potiphar cast eyes upon him,
and wished to sleep with him, but Joseph would not.
Daily she tried to lure him into bed,
and one day grasped his coat, but Joseph fled,
leaving the coat, and then the woman called
to bring the other men, accusing Joseph
of harassment, and they believed her word.
So Potiphar was told and he ensured
that Joseph was confined to gaol, but there
Joseph found favour and became a power
for good among the other prisoners.

IV

ABOUT THAT TIME, a baker and a butler,
who had both worked for Pharaoh, were imprisoned;
and they were in the care of Joseph, who
was able to interpret dreams for them.
One morning Joseph noticed they were sad
and they explained they had experienced dreams
but could not fathom out their meaning. So
they told their dreams to Joseph who was able,
with God's guidance and help, to interpret them.
The butler in his dream had seen a vine,
three branched, which fruited well, and then he pressed
some grapes into the cup of Pharaoh, and
handed the king the cup of wine to drink.
Joseph then said, *This dream is clear: the vine*

which has three branches means three days, and when
three days have passed you will be butler once
again, and you will serve the king anew.
The butler was impressed, and Joseph asked
if he would seek Pharaoh's favour to release
a man in prison who could fathom dreams.
The baker now retold his dream, in which
he saw himself carrying three basketfuls
of cake upon his head; but the birds pecked
and ate the cakes. So Joseph said, *This means*
that in three days Pharaoh will lift your head
and hang you on a tree for birds to peck
your flesh. Both dreams proved to be true: the butler
was restored while the baker lost his life.

V

NOW JOSEPH was in prison two more years,
and at that time the king had two strange dreams.
In one dream Pharaoh saw seven fat cows
rising out of the River Nile, and then,
seven thin cows emerged and swallowed up
the sleek, fat cows. And Pharaoh dreamed again
and in the dream he saw a stalk of corn
with seven ears all fat and good, but soon
there came another stalk on which there grew
seven thin ears, and these were poor and weak.
The thin ears gobbled up the good, fat ears,
and when the king awoke he thought about his dreams,
but could not readily interpret them,
and neither could the wisest men throughout
the whole of Egypt. Soon the butler heard
about Pharaoh's dilemma, recalling then
the Hebrew man he'd met two years ago
in gaol. The butler told the king about
Joseph and how he could interpret dreams.
Joseph was brought from prison, was allowed
to bathe and shave and was then led to Pharaoh.

VI

PHARAOH asked Joseph to explain his dreams,
and Joseph said, *With help from God I shall*
endeavour to decipher what they mean.
So Pharaoh told Joseph what he had seen,
and Joseph said, *Your dreams are clear to me,*
for God has given me the light to know
these things. The seven cows are seven years,
and so the fat cows signify that
for seven years prosperity will bless
your land, while the thin cows signify
that seven years of famine will then follow.
The seven ears of corn repeat the sign,
the fat ears showing crops will prosper for
that length of years, and the weak ears that grew
show that there will be famine in your land
for seven years to follow. As the sign
has been repeated in two dreams, this means
that God will soon bring this to pass. It seems
to me, your servant, that the wisest thing
to do must be to store up grain while
years of plenty prevail, and then there will
be food for all when famine comes upon
your land. Your people then will surely live.
Pharaoh was pleased with this account and knew
Joseph was guided by the Spirit of his God.

VII

PHARAOH was so impressed by Joseph's skill
and wisdom that he gave him charge of all
the land of Egypt, answering to the king
alone; and Joseph wore a golden chain
around his neck and wore rich and fine clothes;
and Pharaoh gave a chariot to Joseph
and all the people bowed before him when
he drove past. Pharaoh also found a wife
for Joseph, daughter of the priest of On.

Joseph was thirty then, and under his rule
the kingdoms prospered well for seven years.
In every city Joseph stored up grain,
ready to meet the years of famine when
they came, and all the granaries were full.
And Joseph's wife, Asenath, bore two sons
and Joseph called them Ephraim and Manasseh.
The years of famine came and Joseph sold
his grain to those who had no food, and people
arrived from foreign parts to buy the grain.

VIII

JACOB sent Joseph's brothers down to Egypt
to buy some grain, but Benjamin stayed
at home. When the ten brothers came to Joseph
he treated them as strangers, though he knew
them well enough. He said curtly to them,
So where is your tribe from? I think you may
be spies and you have come to try us out.
Joseph's brothers denied that they were spies,
and said they were the sons of Jacob, that
they had a younger brother and that one
was dead. Joseph insisted they were spies
and said they must go home and bring to him
the younger brother. Then they were imprisoned
for three days, when Joseph returned and said,
One of you must remain, and all the others
will take their grain and come back here, and mind
you bring your younger brother Benjamin.
While they were talking, Joseph heard them speak
of their regret at harming him so long
ago, and Joseph wept. Simeon was chosen
to stay behind, the others setting off
for home, loaded with sacks of grain in which
Joseph had placed their payment for the grain.
When they discovered that their money lay
there in their sacks, the brothers panicked for
they were convinced they would be penalised

as thieves. They told their father all their news
and he was much alarmed; but he refused
to let young Benjamin go down to Egypt,
even when Reuben promised his return.

IX

THE FAMINE in the land was grim, and Jacob
resolved to send his sons to Egypt, there
to seek for aid again. Reluctantly
allowing Benjamin to go with Judah,
he also gave his sons a range of gifts
to offer Joseph. Furthermore, he told
the brothers they must give to Joseph all
the money previously brought back, as well
as more than ample funds to pay for grain.
Joseph invited all of them to dine,
and he was moved to meet his brother Benjamin.
The brothers dined with Joseph and he set
them at their ease about the money they
had found hidden within their sacks. But still
Joseph concealed his true identity.
The grain was loaded up, but Joseph told
his steward to replace the money in
their sacks, together with a silver cup
to be put in the sack of Benjamin.
The steward apprehended them as they
were journeying, but they denied that they
had stolen anything, and if the cup
was there then might the guilty man be killed.
So when the cup was found with Benjamin
the brothers tore their clothes, and they were taken
back to the city. After consultation
Joseph decreed that Benjamin should stay
with him as slave, while all the others could
go home. Judah offered to stay instead,
because he feared that Jacob would be so
upset that he might die with broken heart.

X

JOSEPH was now full of emotion, so
he sent away his servants and revealed
himself to all his brothers, who were dumb
at this amazing news. He drew them close
and said, *You sold me long ago to be*
a slave in Egypt, though in God must be
the power that brought me here, for famine struck
and I have saved the people from slow death.
And you, my brothers, all of you, must come,
bringing our father with you to live long
in Goshen, where you will be safe from harm.
So this is Benjamin my youngest brother!
Come here, my lad, and let me hold you close.
Then Joseph wept, embracing every one,
and all began to smile and speak together.

XI

WHEN PHARAOH heard that Joseph's brothers had
arrived in Egypt, he was pleased and said
that they and all their kin were welcome, that
the best land would be theirs. They were sent back
home, loaded with provisions, and all
of them received as gifts, rich festal cloaks.
To Benjamin much more was given, five
fine cloaks and silver; and for Jacob, grain
and ample stores to make the journey down
to Egypt from the land of Canaan. Joseph
warned all his brothers not to quarrel while
they journeyed homewards. Jacob overflowed
with joy when first he heard the news, and then
he doubted in his heart, wondering if
it could be true that Joseph was alive.
But when he saw the many gifts his sons
had brought, he was convinced and set his mind
to go to see Joseph before he died.

XII

JUDAH was sent ahead to plan the move,
and in the land of Goshen met with Joseph;
and when Jacob arrived, Joseph rode
to meet him in his chariot, and both
Joseph and Jacob wept, embracing warmly.
Then Joseph promised he would soon arrange
a meeting with the king to guarantee
that they could graze their flocks in the rich lands
of Goshen. Joseph chose five from among
his brothers, taking them to Pharaoh, who
welcomed the family and asked if Joseph
would choose five men to guard the flocks and herds
of Pharaoh. Then Jacob was brought to meet
the king, who asked how old he was, and Jacob
replied that he was young compared with
his forefathers, that he had now attained
just one hundred and thirty years in age.
Jacob gave Pharaoh his blessing, and the king
allowed the tribes to settle in the land.

XIII

DURING THE FAMINE Joseph sold the grain
that he had saved, and Pharaoh gained more power,
but Jacob and his tribes prospered well.

At last, Jacob grew old and knew he must
soon die, so to his sons he gave his blessing.
When at last Jacob died, he asked if he
could be interred at Machpelah where Isaac
and Abraham were buried. Joseph asked
the king if he could bury Jacob where
he himself had chosen to lie. The king
allowed the family to travel north,
after the time of mourning, so that they
could carry out their father's dying wish.
This was then done with pomp and ceremony,

and with loud lamentation from each clan.

Joseph lived on for many years and knew
the children of his sons, but at long last
he died, and his remains were also carried
north to the land of Canaan where he was laid
to rest in the land promised to his fathers.

MOSES
LEADER OF THE EXODUS

I

THE ISRAELITES in Egypt multiplied
until they were a powerful group of tribes;
but a new king ascended to the throne
of Egypt, one who did not recollect
the name of Joseph; and he ruled with might,
enslaving cruelly the tribes of Israel.
They built huge cities for the king of Egypt,
places like Raamses; daily they were whipped
and forced to labour, yet their numbers grew,
and Pharaoh wished to cull the males,
and so he called the midwives, ordering them
to kill male babies. But the midwives feared
the Lord and made excuses. Pharaoh told
the whole Egyptian people that they must cast
into the Nile each new born son of Israel,
though the daughters were allowed to live.

II

A MAN AND WOMAN, both of Levi's clan,
married and had a son. His mother hid
the child as long as she was able; then
after three months she placed him in a basket
of woven bullrushes all sealed with pitch,
and set the basket in the river, hidden

among some reeds. Pharaoh's daughter came down
to bathe with friends and there they found the child.
Immediately she knew the baby was
a Hebrew, and expressing pity, asked
her maid to take the child out of the river.
The baby's sister was close by, and she
suggested that a nurse might be at hand
among the Hebrew slaves. The princess sent
the girl to find a nurse, and she went straight
to her own mother to explain a way
to keep the baby as her own, though promised
as adopted son to Pharaoh's daughter. So
it was agreed that for a wage the mother
should nurse the boy. And when he grew he was
handed to Pharaoh's daughter as her son.
She gave the name of Moses to the boy.

III

ONE DAY Moses the Prince was walking out
among the Hebrew people, when he saw
an Egyptian man thrashing a Hebrew, and so
he looked around, and seeing no one else,
he killed the bullying Egyptian, then
buried the body in the sand. Next day
he walked around and saw two Hebrew men
fighting, and Moses asked the wrong doer
why he fought so. The man said haughtily,
*Will you then kill me, just as yesterday
you killed that poor Egyptian?* Moses was
afraid and thought he would be tried for murder,
and so he fled to Midian where he stayed.

IV

When Moses went into the desert, he
stayed in the land of Midian. One day
he sat beside a well and seven girls
came up, guiding their father Reuel's flocks.
When shepherds came and drove the girls away,
Moses stood up for them and helped them water
their sheep. Later the girls recounted these events,
and Reuel told them right away to bring
Moses along to share a meal. He came,
and soon decided he would like to stay;
and not long afterwards Moses was married
to Zipporah, the daughter of Reuel, who was
the priest of Midian; and they had a son
whose name was Gershom. Meanwhile Pharaoh crushed
the Israelites and made their labour hard.
But God had seen their plight, and his intent
was to release the Israelites from bondage.

V

Moses was leading Jethro's[1] sheep and reached
Horeb,[2] the holy mountain of the Lord;
and there the angel of the Lord appeared
to him, speaking through flames of fire which lit,
but did not burn, a bush upon the mountainside.
Moses was struck with wonder at this sight
and went to view this strange event more closely;
and from the bush he heard the voice of God
calling his name, and Moses said, *I stand*
before you, Lord. Then God spoke again,
This place is holy; take off your shoes but do
not draw too near. I am the God who spoke
to Abraham, to Isaac and to Jacob.
Moses was awe struck, afraid to look at God.
God said, *I know that now my chosen people*
suffer in Egypt. I have heard their prayers
and they will have a rich land flowing

*with milk and honey. You must go to Pharaoh
to bring my people out of Egypt.* Then Moses
confessed he was not competent to lead
the people out. But God promised his grace
and help. Moses was still uncertain, so
he said, *When I approach the people, what
shall I reply when they ask me your name.*
The Lord said, *I am who I am, and you
must say I AM has sent me to you. This
is my eternal name.* And Moses felt
in heart and soul that he was close to God.

VI

MOSES was instructed firmly by the Lord
to go to meet the Israelites, and tell
them of the revelation he had had
from God. He had to tell them also that
they should go out into the desert lands,
and travel for three days, and there to make
a sacrifice; and they must also take
clothing and jewellery. Moses replied,
*They will not listen to my words, for they
will not believe that you have spoken to me.*
God told him then to take a stick and throw
it on the ground, and when he did it turned
into a snake, and Moses ran away.
But God instructed him to take the snake
by the tail. This he did and then the snake
turned back into a stick. The Lord then told
Moses to thrust his hand into his cloak,
and when he took it out it was as white
as snow, a leper's hand. But when he placed
his hand under the cloak and out again,
his hand returned to normal. *These are signs
for you,* said God, *and if they do not mark
these signs, then take some water from the Nile
and throw it on the ground. There it will turn*

to blood. Yet Moses still complained that he
was not good at speech making, and the Lord
commanded him to use Aaron his brother
as his mouth piece. Moses was happier
at that, and went to tell his father-in-law
of what the Lord had told him he must do.

VII

MOSES AND AARON went to meet the king
and said to him, *The Lord commands that you*
release our people so that they may feast
in honour of his name out in the desert.
And Pharaoh said, *I do not know the Lord*
and will not let your people go. They then
explained that they had met the Lord, who wished
that all his people should travel three days
into the wilderness where they would make
a sacrifice to God. But Pharaoh made
the people stay and forced them all
to work much harder than before. He took
away the straw they used for making bricks.
They had to seek for straw, but still their quota
of bricks remained at the same level. When
they failed to meet the number asked, the king
decreed severe punishments. The people
complained to Moses, who then blamed the Lord
for letting Pharaoh practise evil ways.

VIII

THE LORD commanded Moses to return
to Pharaoh, promising that though the king
would first refuse to free the Israelites;
yet in due course he would be moved by signs
and wonders sent by God. *Go,* said the Lord
and I will make the king perceive you as
the messenger of God, and Aaron will

) 33)

speak out for you. Remember what I said
about the rod changing into a snake.
So Moses went to Pharaoh who then asked
for a miraculous sign to be performed.
Aaron threw down his rod before the king,
which then became a serpent. But the king
brought out his sorcerers and they threw down
their rods which also changed to serpents. Yet,
the rod of Aaron swallowed all their rods,
but even so, the king was adamant.

IX

THE LORD instructed Moses to go back
to Pharaoh and to meet him by the Nile;
and there Moses reminded Pharaoh that
he had not yet obeyed the Lord. And then,
instructed by the Lord, Aaron the priest
stretched out his arms, waving his rod across
the waters of the Nile; and when his rod
made contact with the surface of the river,
the waters turned to blood. The fish all died,
the water was undrinkable and all
the people had to dig for water. But
the king would not be moved because he knew
his own magicians could perform such acts.
The Lord sent many plagues upon the land:
vast swarms of frogs and gnats and flies; disease
among the cattle; boils upon the people;
a storm of hail, and locusts by the million;
and darkness over all of Egypt. Time
on time the king agreed to let the slaves
go out into the wilderness – but time
on time he changed his mind and would not let
the people go. So Moses prayed again
and asked the Lord to use his mighty power.

X

MOSES prepared the people to depart,
expecting help and guidance from the Lord.
He told each house to sacrifice a lamb,
and then to take the blood and sprinkle some
upon the doorposts and the lintel, using
a bunch of hyssop. Next they had to roast
the lambs, to eat that night, leaving no flesh
till morning. He explained that the Lord would
pass over all their houses, saving all
of them from death; but each Egyptian family
would lose the first born child. The people ate
their meal, staffs in their hands, sandals on feet,
ready to go, and eating with due haste.
As well as lamb they ate some bitter herbs
and bread which had no leaven. Then they bowed
their heads in prayer and waited for the sign.
At midnight all the first born in the land
of Egypt died, including Pharaoh's child –
in every house, and even in the herds
of cattle. Pharaoh then allowed the people
of God to journey where they willed; and so,
with many gifts of gold and silver, clothes
and jewels, the Israelites hurried away,
heading towards the wilderness and freedom.

XI

THE ISRAELITES made camp near the Sea
of Reeds,³ but meantime Pharaoh changed his mind
and wished the Israelites were still enslaved.
The king sent men in chariots after them
and all the Israelites were much afraid
and cursed their leader for misleading them.
That night Egyptian chariots came close,
but in the dark confusion reigned, and so
the Israelites were saved. At dawn, led by
the Lord, the tribes began to cross the sea,

for in the strengthening wind the waters parted
and a clear path appeared, with waters piled
on either side as Moses stretched his arm
to point the way. But when Egyptian forces
pursued the Israelites across the sea,
the waters closed upon them, and there
the chariots were stuck, and all the soldiers
were drowned. The Israelites clambered ashore,
all safe and sound, and giving thanks to God
they made their way into the wilderness.

XII

THE ISRAELITES were full of joy and, led
by Moses, sang a song of praise to God;
and Miriam, Moses' sister, also sang
and led the women in a dance of triumph,
shaking their timbrels as they leapt for joy.
Yet their joy turned to sorrow when they found
that on their journey life was hard to bear.
The only water that they stumbled on
was bitter and undrinkable, and so
they made complaint to Moses who was told
by the Lord that there was a certain tree
from which the leaves would make the water sweet.
That water kept them going until they came
to an oasis rich with springs and palm trees.

XIII

THE TRIBES moved on, and life was hard for them
because of lack of food. But Moses had
the guidance of the Lord and knew the ways
of desert living. So he showed them how
the manna covered ground and bush, and how
to eat this sweetest of all foods. And then
he led them to the sea and waited for
the quails, blown off course by the wind, to fall

into their hungry hands, though water still
was short. Yes, life was hard, but Moses had
wisdom from God, and every seventh day
he ordered rest for all the tribes, that they
might turn their thoughts to God in quietness.

XIV

WATER was still in short supply as they
journeyed on through the wilderness,
and once again the people grumbled at
their plight. Moses received the blame because
he was their leader; some believed that God
had now deserted them. So Moses prayed
and asked the Lord for help. Guided by God
he took the elders to the holy mountain
and stopped before a mighty rock. He took
the rod which he had used before, and struck
the rock from which a spring of water then
began to flow. He named the spot Contention
because the people had contended there
with God himself. And so they journeyed on.

XV

THE WIFE OF MOSES and his two young sons
Gershom and Eliezer, stayed with Jethro,
father in law of Moses. Then one day
Jethro decided that they should visit Moses
whose camp was near the holy mountain. After
exchanging news, they sacrificed to God
together with the elders of the tribes
and Aaron, Moses' brother. During his stay,
Jethro observed that Moses spent all day
deciding legal disputes. He suggested
that all the people should be organised
in groups, with elders judging for each group.
When this was done, Moses had time to be

the people's representative before
the Lord, and he could pray for all their needs.
So Jethro then returned to his own home.

XVI

WHILE MOSES and the Israelites were by
the holy mountain Sinai, the Lord
called out to Moses while he stood upon
the mountain top. The Lord said, *You have seen*
my deeds. I brought you here, away from Egypt,
as if on eagle's wings. I wish to make
a covenant with my people. They must be
holy for me, a nation called as priests.
Moses explained the word of God to all
the elders. Then the people were to be
all washed and clean, prepared to hear God's word.
When all was ready, thunder rolled along
the mountain top, and lightning flashed across
the sky; a cloud descended on the peaks
and then a trumpet blast was heard. The Lord
told Moses and his brother Aaron that
they should ascend the mountain, while
the tribes stayed there, forbidden to draw near.

Through Moses God expressed his will and gave
to them commandments they should keep. *You shall*
not have another god apart from me;
you shall not make and worship images
of any kind; you shall not take the name
of God in vain; the Sabbath shall be holy
when you and all your house shall do no work;
honour your parents and embrace long life;
you shall not kill; you shall not take a partner
in adultery; you shall not steal; you shall
not bear false witness; and you shall not covet.
And Moses said, *Fear the Lord and do*
not sin, for he is testing you this day.

XVII

THE PEOPLE promised to obey the word
of God and Moses gathered them before
the altar of the Lord. He raised twelve stones,
one for each tribe, and offerings were made.
Then Moses took some sacrificial blood
and poured it into bowls. He sprinkled blood
upon the altar. Then he read God's laws
and all the people promised to obey
their God. He sprinkled blood upon the people
and said, *Behold the blood of the covenant*
which God has made with you this day.
Moses and Aaron took the seventy elders
up to the mountain top, and there they saw
a clear vision of their God in heaven,
who stood upon a pavement made of sapphire.
Later Moses climbed up the mountain all
alone, remaining there for forty days.

XVIII

WHILE MOSES stayed upon the mountain, all
the people wanted to create a god
of gold; so Aaron gathered ear rings,
melted them down, and made a golden calf.
He built an altar for this so called god
and people brought their offerings. Joshua
was on the mountain with his leader Moses,
and when they came back down, they heard the people
shouting and wondered if there was a war.
Moses was carrying the stones on which
the laws of God were carved, but when he saw
the golden calf he burned with anger, and threw
the stones of testimony to the ground,
and they were broken. Moses took the calf
and ground it into dust, and then he told
his brother Aaron that his sin was great.
Moses called all the people to repent,
and they were stripped of all their ornaments.

XIX

MOSES decided that a tabernacle
should be constructed for their worship. He
asked all the Israelites to bring their gifts:
silver and gold and bronze; material
in blue, scarlet and purple; spices, oil,
acacia wood and hair of goats and skin
from rams; onyx and other stones to trim
the ephod of the priest. The men then made
the tent, a mercy seat, an ark to hold
the laws; a standard lamp, a table for
the sacred bread, a sacrificial altar –
and everything was finely wrought for God.
Moses was pleased with what was made and set
up rules for worship, led by Aaron, helped
by all his sons. The glory of the Lord
entered the tent and filled the sacred place.

XX

THE SACRED TENT was pitched outside the camp
and Moses often meditated there;
the people knew that God was present with
their leader, for the Lord addressed him face
to face, just as a friend would speak to him.
Now Moses asked the Lord if he would bless
the people and himself. The Lord replied
and said that he would go with them, and promised
that he would grant the people of his choice
favour and grace. Then Moses asked the Lord
if he could see his glory, but the Lord
explained that any man who saw him would
not live. But the Lord said to him, *Stand there
within that cleft of rock, and I will let
my glory pass you by, covering you with
my hand; and when I have passed by, you will
behold my back, but not my glorious face.*

XXI

MOSES was called to climb the mountain all
alone, taking two slabs of stone on which
the ten commandments would again be written.
The Lord revealed himself to Moses, passing
before him, saying, *I, the Lord your God,*
am merciful and gracious, slow to anger,
and overflowing with my constant love
and faithfulness; I share my love with thousands,
forgiving sins, iniquities and wrongs;
the guilty will be punished and their sons
and grandsons will feel the effects of sins
they have committed. Moses bowed his head
and worshipped. God made a new covenant
with all the tribes and promised they would have
a land to call their own. When Moses came
down from the mountain top his face was shining
because he had been close to God. He gave
the people the commandments of the Lord,
and they agreed to keep his word. From then,
Moses concealed his shining face by wearing
a veil, except when he was called to go
into the sacred tent to speak again with God.

XXII

SEVENTY ELDERS were selected by the Lord,
and Moses took them to the sacred tent;
Moses there prayed, and then his spirit fell
upon them all and they could prophesy.
Around this time, Aaron and Miriam spoke
against their brother Moses and his marriage
to Zipporah, who was a Cushite. They
were also jealous of his leadership.
All three entered the tent of meeting where
they were informed by God that Moses was
his chosen vessel who was privileged
to see and hear the Lord. Miriam was

then cursed with leprosy, but Moses prayed
for her. Within a week she was made well,
and could return to take her place among
the people. Then the tribes moved on again.

XXIII

MOSES decided that the time had come
to send an expedition to the land
of Canaan, which he thought would be the place
where all the tribes could settle down. He chose
a man from every tribe to go and make
a survey of the land and all its peoples.
When they returned they brought back fruits:
clusters of grapes, and figs and pomegranates.
The land, they said, *all flows with milk and honey,*
but all the people there are fierce and strong.
They warned against invasion, though one man,
called Caleb wished to go directly there,
believing they could conquer all the land.
But no one else agreed, and so the tribes
had to remain in desert lands. They then
complained to Moses, many wishing they
had stayed in Egypt. Moses then prayed to God
and asked for guidance, but the response was
that forty years would have to pass before
they went to Canaan. Of all the men who spied
in Canaan, only Joshua and Caleb would
live long enough to see the promised land.

XXIV

THE ISRAELITES grumbled about their plight,
and they were jealous of the power of Moses.
and Aaron. Moses asked the Lord for help,
and he was told that every tribe should bring
a rod and place it in the tent of meeting,
before the ark of testimony. Then

he was to say that God would mark a rod
to show whom he had chosen. Moses did
what God commanded, and the rods were left
until the following day. When Moses went
to see the rods, the rod of Aaron had
begun to sprout, and buds and blossoms grew
upon the rod; and then ripe almonds clustered
all round the rod. The other rods were given
back to the tribes, but Aaron's rod remained
before the ark, a sign to all from God.

XXV

THE ISRAELITES approached near to Edom,
and tried to cross their land, but entry was
refused, so Moses made his camp beside
Mount Hor. While they were there, his brother Aaron
fell ill and died, and Eleazer took
his father's place as priest. For thirty days
all the tribes mourned. Then they moved on, but yet
again the people moaned, especially about
the fiery snakes whose bites had killed their friends.
So Moses made a snake of bronze and set
it on a pole. Whenever people looked
upon the snake he'd made, they would survive
a serpent's bite. The tribes then journeyed through
the land belonging to the Amorites,
and there they had a victory against
their king, Sihon. who lived in Heshbon. So,
the Israelites took over all that land
and conquered other peoples round about.

XXVI

MOSES appointed Joshua to lead
the tribes in future years, for Moses knew
that he would die in a short time. He spoke

to all the people, warning them to mind
their ways, especially to keep God's law.
He read to them the ten commandments, gave
to them a list of other laws, and told
the tribes to love the Lord their God with heart
and soul and mind, reminding them to love
their neighbours also. Moses climbed the slopes
of Pisgah and from there he viewed the land
which God had promised to their forefathers.
Moses himself would never cross the Jordan
into that land, for he was old. He died
in Moab, his eye undimmed by time, and he
was buried there, the place unmarked. And so,
Joshua, son of Nun now led the tribes.
No prophet since that time has been the equal
of Moses, whom the Lord met face to face.

JOSHUA
VICTORIOUS GENERAL

I

THE LORD was guiding Joshua and told
him that the time had come to cross the Jordan
into the Promised Land. He sent two spies
who went to Jericho and stayed with Rahab,
a prostitute. The king of Jericho
heard there were spies at Rahab's house, and sent
some soldiers to arrest them; but Rahab said
the men had left, though she had hidden them
up on the roof under some stalks of flax.
Later she let them down by a strong rope
out of the window, and she told them how
to hide among the hills until pursuit
died down. Before departure they agreed
to save her when the city fell; and she
was asked to hang a cord of scarlet from
the window to identify her house.
The spies reported back to Joshua

to say the country was afraid of war —
and so invasion plans were made forthwith.

II

THE ISRAELITES approached the River Jordan,
and Joshua commanded priests to lift
the ark and walk into the stream. They stood,
holding the ark, and the flow of water ceased.
There they remained while all the people marched
across the river bed. Twelve men were picked,
one from each tribe, and each took up a stone
to carry with them to their camp. When all
the people had crossed over, Joshua
ordered the priests to come out of the water,
and as they did so, water flowed along
the river bed just as it always had
before. The twelve tribes camped at Gilgal, near
to Jericho, and there they raised the stones
as monuments to mark their river crossing,
that in the future people would recall
the miracle that came about that day.

III

BY JERICHO one day, Joshua had
a vision of a man, sword in his hand,
and Joshua took this as a clear sign
that he would lead his troops to victory.
The city seemed to be impregnable,
but Joshua decided on a plan
to take the place. He told the priests to bear
the ark around the city walls, with men
blowing on seven horns marching before,
and all the army following. For six
days in succession this was done, and on
the seventh day they marched around the town
seven times, not just once, and when the horns

were blown after the seventh circuit, all
the people shouted like a roar of thunder,
and at that sound the city walls fell down.
The army captured men and booty, all
devoted to the Lord, but Rahab was
rescued from death because she helped the spies.
The city was in ruins and the Israelites
knew that the Lord was with them on that day.

IV

THEN JOSHUA despatched an expedition
to Ai, a nearby city, but the force
was beaten off and many men were killed.
This great disaster was ascribed to one
who stole from treasures given to the Lord –
a rich cloak, gold and shekels of silver. This
was Achan, and so he and all his house
were stoned to death. Then Joshua made plans
to capture Ai by stratagem. He sent
some men to hide close to the town; and then
he led another group towards the gates.
The men of Ai came out to fight this force,
thinking that victory would soon be theirs.
Then Joshua stretched out his arm to point
his javelin towards the town, at which
the hidden force ran out to capture it.
They then set fire to Ai and slaughtered all
the people, but the king was hung to show
his shame to all the world. An altar then
was raised with unhewn stones, and all the tribes
worshipped the Lord. The law was read to all
the people, great and small – what Moses had
bequeathed to them, with blessing and with curse.

V

THE ISRAELITES then conquered all the land,
the land that God had promised, for no man
was able to survive against their might,
and through all perils God was with the tribes.
Then Joshua divided all the land
so that each tribe received a part, except
the Levites who were given cities as
their own from various tribes. For many years
the Israelites experienced peace and rest,
as Joshua grew old and gained in wisdom.
At last he knew his time had come to say
farewell, and so he gathered all the tribes
of Israel. He reminded them of all
their history from Abraham to Moses,
from Moses to the days of victory
when all the land was conquered with God's help.
And then he challenged all the people, asked
them if they would serve God with faithfulness;
and all the people promised that they would,
forsaking other gods, remembering
their fathers and their godly ways. But then,
Joshua said with zeal, *You cannot serve*
the Lord, for he is holy and beyond
your knowing, for indeed you have no faith.
But all the people said with equal zeal,
But we will serve the Lord, we will be his.
Then Joshua replied, *You yourselves*
are witnesses this day to what you have
now promised. And the people said, *Amen,*
we are firm witnesses against ourselves.
Yes, we will serve the Lord; we will obey
his voice and we shall be his chosen race.
At that a covenant was made, a stone
raised up as witness to their promises.
Then every man went home in peace and hope.
When Joshua departed from this life
they buried him in Ephraim where he lived.

DEBORAH AND BARAK
FREEDOM FIGHTERS

LIFE was not smooth for Israel's tribes,
for kings arose among the Canaanites
and they oppressed God's people. But the Lord
raised up strong leaders in the land of Israel
and God was guide to them. At one such time
Deborah led her people to a victory,
when Jabin ruled with cruel power in Hazor.
Deborah called upon a man named Barak,
who lived in Naphtali, to gather men
to fight against the Canaanites at Tabor.
His army waited on the mountainside,
until the Canaanites, led by Sisera
massed in their chariots down below; and then
the Israelites rushed down and won
the day, slaughtering many. But Sisera
escaped and looked for sanctuary with Jael,
a woman of the Kenite clan. She gave
him milk to drink and let him sleep. But then
she drove a tent peg with a hammer through
his skull, and there Sisera died. His lord,
the king of Hazor was defeated by
the Israelites, who lived in peace for years.

GIDEON
SAVIOUR OF HIS COUNTRY

I

ISRAEL was oppressed by Midianites,
Amalekites and other tribes, and they
cried to the Lord for help. Gideon was
chosen by God to lead his people out
against their foes. An angel came to him
and said, *The Lord is with you, man of valour.*
You must deliver Israel from this plight.

But Gideon felt unworthy of this task,
and said so to the angel, who then said,
The Lord will guide and strengthen you, so go
and smite the Midianites. Gideon then
asked for a sign and brought a meal to set
before the angel and was told to place
it on a rock. The angel touched it with
his staff and fire consumed the food. At that,
the angel disappeared, but Gideon knew
that he was called by God, and worshipped there.

II

SO GUIDED BY THE LORD, Gideon went
by night to where the altar raised to Baal
was placed, and pulled it down. He also cut
down the image set beside the altar,
and built instead an altar to the Lord.
The following day the people of the town
found out with ease that Gideon had destroyed
their images, and they decided he
should die. But Joash, Gideon's father would
not hand over his son. He challenged them
and said, *Let Baal contend against us – if*
he truly is a god. And they were silenced.
From that day on Gideon was nicknamed
Contender with the Baal,[4] for he had fought
for God against the falsities of faith.

III

AMALEKITES AND MIDIANITES again
caused trouble on the borders. Some
camped in the Valley of Jezreel, and so,
strong in the Spirit, Gideon summoned men
from several tribes to fight the enemy.
But he was nervous and he wished to have
another sign from God. He prayed and said,
If you are with me Lord, pray give me a sign.

Now I shall place this fleece upon the ground,
and if you cause the dew to wet the fleece
but not the ground, then I shall know that you
are with me to deliver Israel. As
Gideon had asked, the fleece was soaked in dew
at dawn. But Gideon prayed again and asked
the Lord to give a countersign by keeping
the fleece dry, while around it all the ground
would be soaking with dew; and so it came
about at dawn the following day – and now
Gideon was sure God would abide with him.

IV

GIDEON was warned by God that his force
was too large for his purpose. Therefore
he told the people that any who were
afraid should return home, and twenty two
thousand returned, leaving ten thousand men.
Gideon was warned that this was still too large
a force, so he decided on a stratagem.
He asked the men to go to drink some water
that flowed nearby. Those who kneeled down to drink
were separated, as were those who cupped
their hands. The latter group numbered three hundred,
and these were chosen for the enterprise.

V

GIDEON decided that he would reconnoitre
the situation in the camp of Midian,
and took his servant Purah with him. While
there, Gideon overheard a man recount
a strange dream to his friend. During the dream
he saw a round of barley bread which fell
upon his tent, turning it upside down
and flattening it. His comrade thought he could
interpret what his friend had dreamed. He said,

It means the sword of Gideon will have power
to take our camp and all the host of Midian.

VI

GIDEON was heartened by this dream, and said
to his men, *Rise and fight, for Midian will*
be conquered with the help of God. He then
divided his three hundred men in three
groups of a hundred; and to each man he gave
a trumpet and a jar, and in each jar
a torch. He said to them, *Watch what I do,*
and do the same. With me, blow on your trumpets
around their camp and shout, "Fight for the Lord
and fight for Gideon". So when Gideon's troop
sounded their trumpets others did the same.
Then everyone shattered his jar and lit
his torch, and all shouted, *A sword for God*
and for Gideon. At that the enemy
all panicked and they fled. So Gideon called
the tribes together and they all pursued
the Midianites and slaughtered them. Two kings,
Oreb and Zeeb, were caught and killed, and men
carried their heads to Gideon as a trophy.

VII

GIDEON had further victories and he
was asked to be the ruler of all Israel;
but he refused because he knew the Lord
was ruler of his people. Gideon asked
each man to give a golden earring from
his spoil, and from this gold Gideon created
a golden ephod which became an icon
for worship, and a snare for Gideon's house.
At last, Gideon died, leaving behind
seventy sons, and after he had gone
the people turned again to worship Baal.

SAMSON
MAN OF STRENGTH

I

MANOAH and his wife had borne no children,
but then an angel of the Lord appeared
to the poor woman and announced to her,
You shall conceive and bear a son, but drink
no wine and do not eat forbidden food;
and when your son is born he shall not shave
his head, for he will be a Nazarite, and he
will serve his God for life, to fight against
the Philistines. The woman told her husband
of this annunciation and he prayed
to God to ask for guidance. Then again
the angel spoke to both of them and said
what he had said before. Manoah wished
 to offer some refreshment to the angel,
but he refused and said, *An offering*
to God would be appropriate. And then
Manoah asked the angel's name, which he
explained was far too wonderful to know.
Manoah sacrificed to God, and flames
swept up to heaven, taking up the angel.
And so it was that in due course a son
was born and he was named as Samson, who
was blessed by God and guided by the Spirit.

II

WHEN SAMSON grew to be a man, he fell
in love and wished to take as wife a woman
who was a Philistine. His parents did
not like this choice, but he was adamant.
One day as he was on his way to meet
the girl at Timnah, suddenly a lion
sprang out and roared at him. With his bare hands

he killed the lion. Then on he went to meet
the girl. On his way back he saw that bees
had settled in the carcass of the lion,
and Samson ate some honey, saving some
to share at home. Later there was a feast
to celebrate his marriage. Samson set
a riddle for the thirty men who had
been chosen to accompany him: *From out
of an eater there came something to eat,
out of the strong came something sweet.* He said
that if they solved the riddle in the week,
then he would give them all a set of clothes;
but otherwise, they would give him thirty sets
of clothes. Within three days they had not solved
the problem so, with threats, they asked his wife
to find the answer to the riddle. Samson
returned evasive answers, but she wept
continuously and at last he gave
to her the answer to the riddle. When
the week was up the men confronted him
and said, *This is the answer to the riddle:
sweeter than honey nothing is, and what
is stronger than a lion?* Samson well knew
that they had solved the riddle through his wife.
Inspired by the Spirit of the Lord,
he went to Askelon, there slaughtering
thirty strong men. Then he returned to where
his parents lived, and left his wife, who went
to live with the best man, once Samson's friend.

III

SAMSON decided then to call upon
his wife, taking a kid for her. He wished
to go to see her in her room, but his
father in law forbade him to go in.
*I thought you did not like your wife, you see,
and she is with another man. I have
a younger daughter who is fair. Take her*

instead. But Samson burned with fury. Out
he went and caught three hundred foxes which
he placed tail to tail, lighting all of them
with torches. Then the foxes raced around
and all the crops were set on fire. At that
the Philistines came running and they burned
his wife and father. Samson, was incensed
and slaughtered many Philistines. He hid
inside a cleft of rock. His enemies
went into Judah, looking for their foe,
and all the men of Judah were afraid.
They came to Samson, bound him, and took
him to the Philistines, who cheered to see
him bound. But Samson burst his bonds and grabbed
the jaw bone of an ass and with it killed
a thousand men. He sang triumphantly,
but had a mighty thirst, so the Lord showed
him where to find some water in a hollow.
He judged in Israel during twenty years.

IV

NOW SAMSON fell in love again and he
was captivated by Delilah. She
was bribed by Philistines to find the secret
of his great strength. She asked him what the source
of his power was. He said, *If you secure
me with seven fresh bowstrings, then I shall
lose all my strength.* She did just that and had
some Philistines waiting outside. She called,
Samson, the Philistines are here! He snapped
the bonds with ease and freed himself. He told
Delilah next that seven unused ropes
would do the trick. And then that if his hair
was woven with his seven locks all pinned,
he would soon lose his might. But none of these
provided Samson's secret; so she nagged
him day by day until he broke and told
her that his strength would fade if ever he

shaved his head. She informed his enemies
and while he slept, head on her lap, she had
a man shave off his hair. The Philistines
then seized him and gouged out his eyes. They bound
him and transported him to Gaza where
he had to slave in prison at the mill.
But gradually his hair grew long again
and he began to pick up his lost strength.

V

THE PHILISTINES gathered together so
that they could praise their god, Dagon by name.
They were rejoicing, for their enemy,
Samson, was in their hands. After a time
of drunken merriment, they sent some men
to bring out Samson so that they could make
a clown of him. They made him stand between
two pillars which carried the weight of all
the building. Thousands watched the sport, and some
were on the roof to gain a better view. Then Samson
prayed to the Lord for strength and grasped the two
pillars on which the building stood. He leaned
against the pillars, right and left, and said,
Let me die with these Philistines. He then
pushed mightily and brought the building down.
Thousands of Philistines were killed, and thus
he slew more at his death than in his life.
His family came down and took his body
and laid him in his father's silent tomb.

RUTH
A WOMEN OF LOVE AND LOYALTY

I

A MAN OF JUDAH emigrated, going
to Moab with his wife and their two sons,

Mahlon and Chilion. Their father died,
leaving a widow, Naomi by name.
The two sons married Ruth and Orpah, girls
of Moab; but unhappily the two
sons died, so Naomi had lost her sons
in addition to her husband. She resolved
to go back home to Bethlehem and told
the wives of both her sons to stay in Moab
with hopes of marrying again. Orpah stayed,
yet only after shedding many tears;
but Ruth decided to accompany
Naomi homewards, promising to live
with her through every chance of life. At last
they came to Bethlehem where sympathy
for Naomi was strong. When they arrived
the barley harvest was about to start.

II

NAOMI had a kinsman in the town
whose name was Boaz, a wealthy man. Now Ruth
asked Naomi if she could glean some corn,
and so she followed after those who reaped
within the field of Boaz, who noticed her
and asked his servant who she was. On learning
she was related to his family
by marriage, Boaz spoke to her and told
her to glean only in his field. She thanked
him warmly, bowing to the ground and Boaz
said that he knew of her firm loyalty
and love for Naomi. At mealtimes he
invited her to join his group. He told
his men to let her glean among the sheaves
without rebuking her. When she reached home,
Naomi asked about the work she'd done
that day. So Ruth explained about the favours
bestowed by Boaz. Naomi thanked the Lord
and advised Ruth to glean only with Boaz.

III

NAOMI said to Ruth, *Go now to Boaz*
who will be barley winnowing tonight.
Wash and anoint yourself before you go;
wear your best clothes and wait until he has
finished his meal. When he lies down, uncover
his feet and lie down also. He will tell
you what to do. Ruth did what she was told.
At midnight Boaz wakened. When he turned,
he saw this woman lying at his feet
and said, *Who then are you?* So Ruth replied,
Ruth is my name; I am your servant. Please
cover me with your skirt, for you are next
of kin to me. Now Boaz was delighted
at this development but said to her,
There is another kinsman closer than
I am. I must approach him and if he
accepts responsibility, then so
be it. If not, than I shall do my part.
When morning came, Ruth went away before
she could be recognised, but not before
Boaz had given her a generous measure
.of barley as a gift for Naomi,
who said to her, *Boaz will act today.*

IV

NOW BOAZ sat beside the city gate
and waited till the next of kin came by;
and when he did he said to him, before
the elders of the town, *Naomi has*
some land to sell. You are the next of kin.
Will you redeem the land? At first the man
agreed he would redeem it, but when Boaz
explained that Ruth had also to be bought,
the man decided not to act as next
of kin, inviting Boaz to take his
place as redeemer. Boaz said he would,

and gave the man his sandal as a bond.
So Ruth of Moab married Boaz, all
the elders being witnesses. In time,
Ruth bore a son she named as Obed, who
became father of Jesse, who became
father of David, famed king of all Israel.

SAMUEL
PROPHET AND KING MAKER

I

HANNAH was childless, though Elkanah's other
wife was a mother, and poor Hannah was
distraught. Each year he went to Shiloh so
that he could sacrifice to God. On that
occasion he shared out the meal, but gave
Hannah a single helping, while the other
wife and children had the lion's share.
Hannah was sad and often wept at her
predicament, although her husband loved
her. After one such meal, Hannah prayed long
that God would give her children. Eli,
who was the priest at Shiloh, watched her pray
and thought that she was drunk because she prayed
in silence, though her lips were moving. When
the priest came up to her, Hannah denied
that she was drunk, saying that she was hurt
by circumstance. The priest said, *May your prayer
be granted*. Hannah went away, her heart
at peace. A short time afterwards, it came
about that Hannah bore a son. When he
was weaned she took him to the temple where
she told the priest how her prayer had been
answered by God. She said to Eli, *This
my son is given to the Lord for life*.
And so the child remained with Eli there.
Hannah gave praise to God with her own song.
 My heart exults in the Lord;

my strength is exalted in the Lord.
My mouth derides my enemies,
because I rejoice in thy salvation.[5]

II

THE SONS OF ELI cheated those who came
to make a sacrifice and they were not
acceptable to God. But Samuel
was young and innocent and served the Lord
most faithfully; his mother too was blessed
and bore two daughters and three other sons.
Now Eli was beginning to grow old
but Samuel was growing in God's favour
and gained in reputation among men.
A man of God came in one day to see the priest
and said to Eli that his sons were doomed
because they did not keep God's law. And more,
he prophesied that God would raise a priest
of great integrity to serve him there,
a priest who would express the will of God
in all he thought or did, a priest who would
have a sure place in Israel's history.

III

THE WORD OF GOD was rare in Eli's time,
when Samuel was young, but Samuel
had special insights. Now one night, when he
was sleeping in the temple, where the ark
was standing, while the lamp of God was still
alight, he heard a voice calling to him,
the Lord's voice, though he did not realise
that it was God who called out, *Samuel!*
Samuel! He replied, *Yes, here I am,*
and ran to Eli, who then said, *It was*
not I who called. Go back to sleep. The boy
lay down again, but then he heard the voice

calling once more, but Eli still maintained
he had not summoned Samuel. But when
the voice called Samuel for the third time,
Eli at once knew that the Lord was calling.
He said to Samuel, *Lie down again,*
and if you hear the voice, then you must say,
'Lord speak, for I am here.' And listen well
to what the Lord is saying. So the boy
lay down and did as was told. And God
told him that Eli's house was doomed because
his sons had sinned. But Samuel grew up,
respected as a prophet in the land.

IV

THE PHILISTINES defeated Israel, slaying
many, and so the elders sent some men
to bring the ark, which was borne by the sons
of Eli. All the tribes shouted thankfully,
for with the ark a victory would soon
be theirs – or so they thought. The Philistines
were much afraid because they thought the ark
was surely a god; but still they set their minds
to fight with all their courage. When the fight
was started, soon the Philistines began
to triumph, and the Israelites were slain
in thousands. Moreover the ark was lost
and carried off. A messenger arrived
in Shiloh with the awful news that both
of Eli's sons were dead. The old man fell
at this grave shock and broke his neck. Then his
daughter in law gave sudden birth and bore
a son, whom she called Ichabod[6] because
all glory had departed from the land.

V

THE PHILISTINES set up the ark beside
Dagon, their god; but morning brought a shock,
for Dagon lay face down upon the ground.
They lifted up their image, placing him
beside the ark again; but morning found
their god shattered to pieces, arms and head
cut off, and leaving but the trunk. Around
that time the Philistines were troubled by
disease, especially where the ark was kept;
and when the ark was moved from town to town,
so the disease followed and their fear grew.
They then decided that the ark must go.
Accordingly, advised by priest and sage,
they loaded up the ark onto a cart,
and sent it back, drawn by some cows. Beside
the ark they placed some golden images
to take away their guilt. Some harvesters
spotted the ark which the cows drew, and watched
as it came to a halt near a huge stone.
The Israelites broke up the cart and used
the wood to sacrifice the cows. The ark
was placed within the house of Eleazar,
at Kiriath-jearim where it stayed in care
for twenty years. The Israelites lamented
at their sad plight, and longed to know the Lord.

VI

SAMUEL called all Israel to repent
and gathered all the tribes at Mizpah, where
the Israelites confessed their sins and held
a fast. The Philistines became aware
of this assembly and decided that
they would attack – so all of Israel was
afraid. The people prayed that Samuel
should intercede for them, and so he took
a lamb and offered it to God, and prayed

with heart and soul, and the Lord answered him.
The Philistines were routed and, when peace
was gained, Samuel raised a monument
and called it *Stone-of-help*. The Israelites
regained lost territory, and all the days
of Samuel, justice and peace held sway.

VII

WHEN SAMUEL grew old, his sons became
judges in Israel, but they were corrupt,
and all the elders came to Samuel
to ask that there should be a king to rule
the land. When Samuel prayed to the Lord
about this matter, he was told that such
a step would not be pleasing, for the Lord
himself was king. So Samuel explained
to those who pressed their case, that a king's ways
would be oppressive, and that he would take
their sons as soldiers, and their daughters as
his servants; and he would expect a share
of crops, would commandeer animals
to labour in his fields. But Israel wished
to have a king and would not change their minds.
So Samuel prayed yet again, and God
instructed him to let the people have
their way, to have a king to rule in Israel.

VIII

A MAN CALLED SAUL went looking for his asses
which had been lost. Despondent, he made up
his mind to go to Samuel the seer
and prophet. Samuel had been forewarned
a future king would come to see him. When
he perceived Saul, he knew he was the man
the Lord willed to be king. When Saul enquired
about his asses, Samuel told him

they had been found; but also asked if Saul
would dine with him, and Saul stayed all night. At dawn,
when Samuel went with Saul to the edge
of the town, Samuel anointed Saul with oil
and told him that he would be king. Then Saul
consorted with some prophets and began
to prophesy, for God's own Spirit came
with might upon him. Samuel then called
the tribes to Mizpah where he wished to make
Saul king. But Saul had hidden out of shyness,
despite his towering height and massive strength.
At length they found him and he was anointed.
The people shouted, *May the king live long!*
Then Samuel explained the rights and duties
of a good king, and in a book his words
were saved before the Lord for all to read.

IX

Now Samuel realised that he
was getting old, and so he gathered all
the people and admonished them because
they had been faithless to the Lord. He prayed
for them, and God sent thunder and much rain,
and then the people were afraid of God,
and promised they would change their ways. He warned
them that if they should fall away again,
the Lord would judge them for their sin. Now Saul
and Samuel had differences, for Saul
would not obey God's word, and Samuel
revealed that Saul's kingdom would end because
of his self pride. The Philistines began
to take control, and it was they who had
the smiths to deal with metal. Israel was
deprived of weapons while their enemies
grew strong. But Saul's son, Jonathan,
performed an exploit which created panic
among the Philistines, and therefore Saul
his father was victorious. The tribes,

then fought against the feared Amalekites,
and Saul their king, ordered by Samuel,
led all his forces into battle. Saul
defeated the Amalekites; but when
their king was captured he did not obey
the ban, and he allowed Agag their king
to live. When Samuel arrived he was
displeased and used his sword to kill Agag
himself. Then Saul confessed his sin, but when
he grasped the robe of Samuel, he tore
the hem; and Samuel turned round and said,
As you have torn my robe, so your reign will end
and the Kingdom of Israel will be torn
from you. From that day onwards Samuel
did not see Saul again before his death.

X

NOW SAMUEL was guided by the Lord
to go to see Jesse of Bethlehem,
there to identify a future king
among his sons. The elders in the town
were fearful when the prophet Samuel
appeared, but he announced that he had come
in peace to make a sacrifice. He asked
Jesse to bring his sons along. When they
arrived the prophet looked at seven sons,
but not one was acceptable to God,
who looks beyond the superficial man.
Samuel said, *Have you no other son?*
At that, the youngest son was brought, for he
had been watching the sheep. Now David had
beautiful eyes and fresh complexion. He
was chosen by the Lord. Samuel then
took up the horn of oil, anointing David,
who from that day was guided by the Lord
and mightily inspired by the Spirit.
But Saul had lost the Spirit of the Lord.

DAVID
FOUNDER OF A DYNASTY

I

KING SAUL was often troubled, and he heard
that David was an expert with the lyre;
so forthwith he sent for David who brought
gifts from his father, Jesse. David soothed
the king's spirit with music, and the king
took David into service, and he loved
the boy so much that David soon became
the armour bearer of the king. Now round
this time, the Philistines were strong, and one
of them, Goliath, was gigantic. He
decided to issue a challenge, calling
for an opponent from the Israelites.
Saul and his men were frightened at this move,
for Goliath's spear was like a weaver's beam,
his armour weighty and strong, his helmet made
of bronze. Goliath called again and said,
If one of you can conquer me, then we
shall be your servants; but if I prevail,
then you shall be our slaves. David had brothers
in Saul's army, and he was sent with food
from home to give to them. While he was there,
Goliath issued yet again his challenge,
and David scorned the Philistine. Saul heard
of this and sent for David, telling him
he was too young to fight. But David said,
The Lord has helped me to defeat a bear,
and I have fought with lions, and he will
empower me to defeat Goliath.

II

DAVID tried on the armour of the king,
but felt uncomfortable, so he took
the armour off and armed only with staff

and sling set out to face Goliath. From
a stream he chose five smooth stones, putting them
into his wallet. When Goliath perceived
a fresh faced youth coming to challenge him,
he cursed and laughed disdainfully. At that,
David spoke out and said, *You have both sword
and spear, but I have come in the Lord's name,
and I will knock you down and cut your head off!
You Philistines will perish and the birds
and beasts will feast upon your flesh, and all
the earth will see that he is Lord and God.*
The Philistine drew near and David ran
to meet Goliath, stone in sling, and threw
the stone and hit the giant on the forehead.
Goliath fell, face to the ground; and then
David drew out the giant's sword and hacked
his head off. When the Philistines saw this,
they fled and all the Israelites arose
and cheered, then chased the Philistines as far
as Gath. David then took the severed head
of the slain giant into Bethlehem.

III

DAVID stayed on at court and became a friend
to Jonathan, who gave to David clothes
and armour and a sword. Now Jonathan
was Saul's loved son and the two youths expressed
their friendship in a covenant. It came
about that David was soon famous as
a soldier, and the people praised him more
than Saul. They used to sing,

> *Saul has slain his thousands,*
> *and David his ten thousands.*

The king was jealous and was then possessed
by evil; and one day when David played
his lyre, Saul threw his spear, but David moved
quickly aside and saved his life. So Saul
arranged for David to become a captain

over a thousand soldiers, and he left
the court. David had great success and all
Israel loved him and stood in awe of him.

IV

SAUL offered Merab to be David's wife,
but marriage to this daughter of the king
was cancelled and she married some one else.
Saul's other daughter, Michal, later fell
in love with David, and Saul was pleased at this
development and set a trap for David. When
Saul's messengers came to speak to David
about a marriage, he declared he was
not worthy and was also poor. But Saul
sent further word, suggesting that no gift
from David would be sought, except that he
should bring the king a hundred foreskins from
the Philistines he slew. Thus, Saul had hopes
that David would be killed. So David did
what was required, and more, by slaughtering
two hundred Philistines. When David had
presented all the foreskins[7] to King Saul,
the wedding then took place. But Saul knew well
that all the people loved his son in law,
and that the Lord was with him. Therefore
King Saul's hatred increased and from then on
he was for ever David's enemy.

V

JONATHAN spoke to Saul about his friend,
David, and Saul let David stay at court,
promising not to do him harm, but when
David again won battles and enhanced
his name, Saul tried to kill him but, with help
from Michal, David fled and went to live
with Samuel. Then David went to see

the priest, a man called Ahimelech who,
despite his worries, gave some holy bread
to David, who was hungry. David asked
if Ahimelech had a sword to spare,
and the priest gave him Goliath's sword.
David then went to Gath, one of the towns
which Philistines inhabited. The king
was warned by men against David, who feigned
madness. King Achish scorned David who once
again moved on, and formed an outlaw band.

VI

FOR SAFETY David's parents went to Moab;
his brothers joined him with four hundred men.
Saul slaughtered Ahimelech and his priests,
though Abiathar managed to escape
and fled to David, who saved him from harm.
King Saul pursued David, high and low,
in valley and on mountain, but he could
not capture him. He went into a cave
one day, in order to relieve himself.
David was in the cave, but did not kill
the king, but he cut a strip from the cloak
of Saul by stealth. Later he told the king
of how he'd had him in his power, and Saul
was moved to weep at his own wickedness.
He said to David, *Now I know that you
will one day take the crown of Israel. Vow
to me that you will not cut off my sons.*
So David swore that this would be his care,
and each man went his way with heart at peace.

VII

A MAN CALLED NABAL had much land and flocks
of sheep, and David sent some men to ask
the man for food for all his men, for David

had guarded Nabal's shepherds in the fields.
But Nabal was ill tempered and refused
to help, so David thought he would avenge
himself upon the man and gathered arms
and many men. But Abigail, the wife
of Nabal, heard of this and loaded beasts
with grain and wine and figs and meat, along
with raisin clusters, and she met with David
and begged forgiveness for her husband. Now
Abigail was beautiful and wise and she
persuaded David to accept her way.
So David and his men went home. That night
a feast was held by Nabal, who was drunk
with wine. It was next morning when he was
informed of Abigail's presents to David
and he was apoplectic and he died
within ten days. When David heard this news,
he sent for Abigail and married her.
He also took another wife, though Michal
was given by her father to another.

VIII

DAVID AND ABISHAI entered the camp
of Saul by night, when all the men were sound
asleep. They found King Saul, also asleep,
his spear at his head. Then Abishai
offered to slay the king, but David would
not harm the Lord's anointed king. Instead,
they took Saul's spear and his jar of water,
and then crept stealthily away. At dawn
David shouted to Abner from a hill
across the valley, taunting him because
he had not guarded Saul his king. *Look here,*
called David, *I have taken Saul's own spear
and jar of water.* Saul came out and said
to David, *I have done wrong. No more harm
will come to you.* David said he would
return the spear. Saul then gave his blessing

and said that David would have great success
in all he did. So both men went their way.

IX

NOW SAMUEL had died, and Saul was left
without the prophet's guidance. Mediums
and wizards were forbidden by the king
to practise magic arts. The Philistines
were growing in their power and Saul was much
afraid. His prayers for guidance were not answered,
so he sought out a medium, the witch
of Endor. He disguised himself and went
to find the woman one dark night. He said
to her, *Bring me the spirit of the one
whose name I give to you.* The woman was
reluctant, for she knew her arts were now
against the law. But after threats she then
agreed to do what Saul required, which was
to conjure up the form of Samuel.
The woman did as she was told, and Saul
believed he saw the ghost of Samuel.
Saul asked for Samuel's advice about
the threat of Philistine aggression, but
the ghostly voice declared that Saul would be
defeated and that he would die. At that,
Saul was deeply afraid and would not eat,
but the old woman and his men persuaded
him to take food to bolster up his strength.

X

DAVID had joined the Philistines and lived
with them as friends, under the care of Achish.
But when the Philistines gathered for war
against the Israelites, David was made
to stay behind, for it was thought he might
re-join the army of the Israelites.

The armies met at Mount Gilboa, where
the Israelites were vanquished. Jonathan
and other sons of Saul were slain. Now Saul
was badly wounded by some archers, so
Saul told his armour bearer to slay him there,
but the man would not do the deed, so Saul
fell on his sword and killed himself, with help
from an Amalekite, and so too died
the armour bearer. When the Philistines
found Saul, they severed off his head and hung
his body on a wall. Some Israelites
were brave enough to take the body, which
they later burned with reverence and respect.

XI

WHEN DAVID heard the news about the death
of Saul and Jonathan, he was much grieved.
He asked the man who brought these tidings what
had happened; and the man explained that Saul
had asked for help to die. The man had brought
the royal crown and armlet. Later that day
David asked the Amalekite why he
had dared to slay the Lord's anointed. Then
the messenger was slain. But David wrote
a sad lament about the deaths of Saul
and Jonathan. From there he made his way
to Judah where the people made him king
at Hebron, and he reigned there seven years.

XII

THE TRIBES OF ALL OF ISRAEL came to David
and asked if he would be their king; and so
King David covenanted with the tribes,
and was anointed king of Israel. David wished
Jerusalem to be his capital,
and though it was believed to be impregnable,

{ 71 }

he captured it by clever stratagem.
There he built a palace with the help
of Hiram, king of Tyre, whose men were skilled.
Then David was beset by Philistines,
but with the help of God he conquered them.
He then decided that the ark should be
set in Jerusalem to mark God's presence.
Despite a setback this was brought about,
and David's men processed before the ark,
and David danced with joy to lyre and harp.
His first wife Michal, now returned to him,
despised him for his merry dance and told
him so. But she was childless to her death.

XIII

KING DAVID said to Nathan, *We must build
a house for God. I myself dwell in a house,
so how much more should God be housed in splendour?*
At first, Nathan agreed, but in the night
he had a dream in which the Lord revealed
to him that David should not build a house
for God. Nathan explained to David that
the Lord had always lived in a tent, and so
he wanted to remain, as when the tribes
lived in the wilderness. But Nathan said,
*The Lord will build a house for you and all
your seed for ever; and your son will build
a house for him. The Lord will say to him:
"I will be his father, and he shall be
my son, but if he sins he will be punished;
but yet I shall not take my steadfast love
away from him. Your dynasty will be
made sure for ever."* David's soul was stirred
and he went to pray alone, praising his God.

XIV

THE LORD gave David many victories
and he became both rich and powerful,
though constant wars went on. But David stayed
within Jerusalem. One afternoon
he walked across the roof of his own house,
and down below he saw a woman bathing,
and David made enquiry to his men
about her, for she was most beautiful.
David was told that she was wife to one
of David's officers, Uriah, who
was of the Hittite race, and was at war
on Israel's side. David seduced Bathsheba
and made her pregnant, so the king sent word
to Joab, general of the army, that
he should despatch Uriah home. The king
feigned friendliness, then tried to trick the man,
persuading him to go home to Bathsheba;
but when Uriah would not break his vow
of abstinence, the king sent him away,
back to the war. He gave the man a note
to give to Joab, ordering that he
should make Uriah fall in battle by
abandoning the man when fighting hard.
And so Bathsheba married David, but
the prophet Nathan heard of this
and made the king repent his wickedness.
Bathsheba's child did not survive, but she
produced a son whose name was Solomon.

XV

KING DAVID had a son called Absalom
and loved him much. But then Absalom killed
another royal son because he raped
his sister, Tamar. Absalom ran off,
a fugitive, to live in Geshur. David
was saddened by this loss, but Joab sent

for Absalom, when David had agreed;
and Absalom returned, but had to live
apart from David. Absalom was fair
to look upon and had four children. He
implored his father to allow him back
at court, and David gave permission. Yet
Absalom made himself favoured among
the populace, and he designed to take
the crown. He gathered men at Hebron who
supported him, so David had to flee,
taking the ark and both chief priests, and all
his faithful followers. But King David was
astute, and sent a man to Absalom
to spy on him. He also sent the ark
back to Jerusalem along with Zadok
and Abiathar, priests of the Lord. Then David
 travelled across the River Jordan; but
Absalom followed with his men. The two
armies then engaged, though David told
his chiefs to capture Absalom alive.
David defeated Israel, slaughtering many,
and Absalom was killed deliberately
at Joab's hand. David was moved at this
and wept in private. Then at last he gained
his throne again and took Jerusalem.

XVI

DAVID was old and needed care. On that
account a nurse was brought to be with him.
She even slept with him to keep him warm,
but David did not have sex with the girl,
despite her beauty. At this time, a son
of David's, Adonijah, wished to be king.
He had support from Abiathar, but
Zadok the priest and Nathan were against
him. Nathan went to see Bathsheba, and warned
her of this plot, and said that Solomon,
her son, would be the king of Israel. She

went to see David, Nathan joining her.
The king agreed that Solomon should be
successor to the throne. It was arranged
that Solomon should be anointed by
Zadok the priest beside the river Gihon,
and all the people shouted, *May the king
live long; long live king Solomon!* There was
a time of great rejoicing in the land of Israel.
The disappointed Adonijah sought
for sanctuary by the altar, but
King Solomon forgave him at the time.
Before his death, King David charged his son
to keep the laws of Moses and to rule
wisely. When David died he had been king
for forty years and he had written songs
and psalms which witness to his love of God.

SOLOMON
THE WISE

I

THE REIGN OF SOLOMON began with blood
being shed. Adonijah asked if he
could marry Abishag, the girl who nursed
King David when he needed care. This was
taken by Solomon to be a slur
upon his father's name, and Adonijah
was killed. So too was Joab killed because
he had supported Adonijah. Then
the chief priest, Abiathar, was expelled
and made to live within his own estate,
and others, too, were punished. Solomon
made treaties with the powerful, and took
in marriage Pharaoh's daughter. There was no
temple as yet, so Solomon and all
the tribes made sacrifices to the Lord
at ancient sanctuaries in the hills.

II

THE LORD appeared to Solomon by night,
and in this dream the Lord asked Solomon
what gift he should be given. The king said,
Now I am in the place of David, but
I am a little child in wisdom, so
I pray that you will make me wise to rule
your chosen people well. The Lord agreed
that this should be his gift, and so the king
was able to discern evil from good.
One day two harlots came to see the king
and asked if he could solve a dispute. Both
of them laid claim to the same child, which had
 been born some days before, another child
then born having died. Now when Solomon
considered these two claims, he thought a test
would solve the problem. So he said to them,
With this sharp sword I shall divide this child
and each of you will take one half. One woman
agreed to this, but the other one said,
Give her the baby: do not kill this child.
So Solomon perceived which woman loved
the baby, and gave it to the woman who
protected it. All Israel heard of this
and praised their king for being so wise a judge.

III

KING SOLOMON brought peace to all the land,
and he could muster many chariots
and fighting men. His court was always filled
with people, and all his food supplies
were drawn from round the country. Even so,
men had their vines and fig trees under which
they sat contented. Solomon was both
poet and sage, writing proverbs and songs
about experience and the world of nature.
After a time, Solomon recalled

that David had not built the temple he
had planned, and so the king made up his mind
to raise a glorious temple to the Lord.
Hiram of Tyre supplied materials and men
to do the work, while Solomon agreed
to give to Hiram wheat and oil. The two
kings made a treaty and they lived in peace.
The temple was magnificent for worship
and there the ark of covenant was set
apart within the holy sanctuary

IV

THE QUEEN OF SHEBA heard of Solomon,
especially of his wisdom, and she came
to find if all that she had heard was true.
She had a splendid retinue and brought
spices and precious stones and gold. She asked
the king hard questions, but he answered all
she wished to know. The wisdom of the king
and all his wealth astounded her and she
was low in spirit. Then she blessed the king
and gave him many gifts. The king returned
her acts of kindness with his own, and gave
to her whatever she desired of him.
Traders from many parts brought wealth and power
to Solomon. He had a throne inlaid
with ivory and many shields of gold;
and all the vessels in his house were made
of gold. He had a fleet of ships which sailed
to Tarshish and elsewhere, and these returned
with gold and silver, ivory and apes
and peacocks. Solomon excelled in his
magnificence above all other kings.

V

NOW SOLOMON had seven hundred wives
and kept three hundred concubines. His wives
persuaded him to worship many gods,
and in this way he broke God's covenant.
His enemies arose and attacked him,
and so he had to go to war. Even in Israel
a man called Jeroboam, guided by
a prophet called Ahijah, took ten tribes,
though not until King Solomon had died.
This left his son with but a part
of his old kingdom. Altogether he
was king for forty years and when he died
his son, a cruel ruler, took the crown.
From then the kingdoms were divided, north
and south, Israel and Judah, and David's sons
had but a small region under their rule.

ELIJAH
THE PROPHET

I

ELIJAH prophesied to Ahab, king
of Israel that the Lord would send a drought
upon the country for three years. The Lord
guided the prophet, sending him to hide
beside the River Cherith, far away,
east of the Jordan. There he lived, and ravens
fed him with scraps of meat. After a time
the brook dried up because there was no rain.
The Lord then told Elijah that he must
travel to Zarephath in Sidon. There
he met a widow gathering sticks, and asked
for food and drink. She used her last resource
of oil and meal to feed herself, her son,
and the strange man she had just met. From then,
supplies of oil and meal were always there,
just as Elijah had foreseen. One day

{ 78 {

the widow's son fell ill, and seemed to die.
Elijah took the boy and three times stretched
himself upon him. By the power of God,
the boy revived, and the old woman said,
By this I know that you were sent by God,
and that the word of God is in your mouth.

II

ELIJAH met the king again and asked
if he would gather all the prophets bound
to Baal and Asherah upon Mount Carmel.
The people too assembled and Elijah
exhorted them to choose between the Lord
and Baal. The people sat in silence, so
Elijah said, *Now let Baal's prophets set*
a pile of wood ready to light, and I
shall do the same; and we shall lay a bull
on each. Then we shall pray to see if God
or Baal will send down fire from heaven to light
the sacrifice. Baal's prophets acted first,
and danced and cried to Baal, but no fire came.
They raved and raved beyond midday, but still
no fire descended from above. So then
Elijah raised an altar to the Lord
and placed some wood upon it, and the bull
for sacrifice; and then he dug a trench
and poured gallons of water on the wood.
Elijah prayed then to the Lord, the God
of Abraham, Isaac and Jacob. From
above, the fire of God fell down upon
the sacrifice, consuming it in flames,
and licking up the water. All the people
then turned against Baal's prophets and the king
was bowed in shame. Elijah told the king
that rain would fall to end the drought. Elijah
watched with his servant from the mountain top,
and at long last the rain fell heavily,
and the long drought was broken by God's word.

III

NOW THE QUEEN, Jezebel, was furious
at what Elijah had achieved, and she
threatened to kill the prophet. Guided by
an angel voice, Elijah fled and went
to Mount Horeb, and lived within a cave,
high on the mountainside. There he complained
to God about his plight, believing he
only was faithful to God. He went outside
the cave and stood before the Lord, and felt
the Lord pass by. A mighty wind began
to blow, but God was not within the wind.
Earthquake and fire then came, but God was not
in them. At last, from a great silence came
the still, small voice of God. Elijah stood
and waited for the Lord to speak. And God
assured the prophet that among the people,
seven thousand were faithful to God and had
not worshipped Baal. The Lord also revealed
that in the times to come Elijah would
anoint Elisha as a prophet. More,
he would anoint kings both in Syria
and Israel. So Elijah found the man,
Elisha, at his plough and called him there
to follow God and prophesy his word.

IV

NOW NABOTH owned a fertile vineyard which
Ahab the king desired to have. The king
offered to buy the vineyard, offering
Naboth a better place. But Naboth wished
to keep the family vineyard and refused
to sell. Ahab began to sulk, and so his wife,
Queen Jezebel, when she had understood
the situation, said she would obtain
the vineyard for the king. She hatched a plot
to frame poor Naboth, and two rogues, in front

of witnesses, said Naboth had cursed both
God and the king. Naboth was stoned to death,
and Ahab took possession of the vineyard.
Elijah, knowing of this wicked plot,
confronted Ahab and foretold that he
would soon be killed. When Ahab heard these words
of condemnation, he tore up his clothes
and wore sackcloth and fasted in dejection.
The prophet's words came true when Ahab died
in war and Jezebel was later murdered.

V

So Ahaziah then became the king
of Israel, but he had a fall and was
confined to bed. He sent some messengers
to ask of Baalzebub, the God of Ekron,
whether he would recover. On their way
they met Elijah who made them go back
to tell the king that he would die because
he had ignored the God of Israel. Then
the king despatched some men to bring Elijah,
but fire consumed them and they died. The same
thing happened when another group approached
the prophet. But the leader of the third
party to go beseeched the prophet not
to let them die. Elijah went with them,
but told the king he would expire because
he had consulted Baalzebub. The prophecy
came true and Ahaziah did not live.
The time came also for Elijah's passing,
and he informed Elisha that he would
depart. Elisha would not leave his master,
and sought a double portion of Elijah's spirit.
Elijah answered, *If you see me when
I go, the Lord will grant your wish.* And so
it came about. Elisha saw the fiery
horses and chariots which came upon
Elijah, taking him to heaven, borne

upon a whirlwind. Then Elisha took
the cloak dropped by his master, and he was
empowered by the Lord to lead the band
of prophets in their work for Israel's God.

ELISHA
THE PROPHET

I

ELISHA was respected as a prophet,
though cheeky boys were wont to call him names.
In Jericho the water spring was bad,
until Elisha salted it and made
it pure. His reputation grew, and when
kings needed help they called upon Elisha
to give advice. The king of Israel and two
allies in war were short of water while
they journeyed, but Elisha prophesied
that water would appear in a dried
up water course, and so it did. And then
he told the kings that victory would come
against the rebel king, Mesha of Moab.
Indeed they won the day, but Mesha took
his son to sacrifice to his own god,
and Israel drew back into their own land.

II

ELISHA often passed through Shunem. There
a woman made a place for him within
her house, where he could stay. The woman had
no child, but then Elisha, wishing her
to satisfy her deepest need, told her
that she would bear a son. This came about
in time, but when the boy had grown he went
to help his father in the fields. One day
he had a head ache. He was taken home

and shortly afterwards he died. When
Elisha heard of this he sent his servant,
Gehazi, who carried the prophet's staff
to lay upon the face of the dead boy.
The boy did not recover, so Elisha
set out himself, and when he saw the boy
he knew what he must do. He lay across
the body, breathing into the boy's mouth,
which warmed the child, who opened his eyes wide
and sneezed seven times. When the woman saw
her son she was astonished, and she bowed
in thanks before Elisha, filled with joy.

III

NAMAAN OF SYRIA was a leper, though
he was a general and reputed brave.
His wife had a young maid, an Israelite,
and the girl told her mistress that there was
a prophet in the land of Israel who
could cure her husband of his leprosy.
The king insisted that his general went
to Israel for a cure. Naaman took much
money and many gifts together with
a letter to the king of Israel from
the king of Syria. But the king of Israel
was upset because he could not heal the man.
Elisha heard of this and told his king
to send Naaman the leper to his house,
where he, Elisha, would provide a cure.
So Naaman travelled to Elisha's house,
but Elisha simply sent a messenger
to tell the general that he ought to go
to wash in the River Jordan seven times.
Naaman was furious at this and went away,
arguing that the rivers at his home
were better than the waters found in Israel.
His servants managed to persuade him that
he should obey the prophet, and he did

as he was asked. He was then cured and went
back to Elisha's house to thank the prophet.
Elisha would receive no gift, but Naaman
promised to worship, from then on, the God
of Israel. But he asked for pardon if
he had to bow to Syria's god when he
returned to service with his king. And so,
Elisha said to him, *Go in God's peace.*
The servant of Elisha, named Gehazi, went
to follow Naaman, asking for some gifts,
pretending they were for Elisha's friends.
Later Elisha taxed him with his gross
dishonesty, and said his punishment
would be to suffer Naaman's leprosy,
and the man's skin became as white as snow.

IV

ELISHA warned the king of Israel what
the king of Syria planned to do in war.
This happened frequently, and so the king
of Syria blamed his men for being spies.
But when he found it was Elisha's doing,
the Syrian king decided he would take
the prophet in the town of Dothan. So
the Syrian army then besieged the town,
and when Elisha rose from sleep he saw
their chariots. Then Elisha's servant was
afraid, but when Elisha prayed, they could
both see the chariots of the Lord around
the town. Elisha prayed again, at which
the Syrians were made temporarily blind.
The prophet led them to Samaria,
promising to lead them to the man
they sought. Thus they were led to meet the king
of Israel, who then wished to kill them. Now
the Syrians' eyes were opened, but Elisha
gave food and drink to them and sent them home.
From then the Syrians did not raid in Israel.

V

LATER THE SYRIANS came again, besieging
Samaria, and in the town the price
of food was very high. The king of Israel
thought that Elisha was to blame for this,
and sent a man to kill the prophet, but
Elisha locked the door. The king arrived
and now blamed God for his predicament.
Elisha said that prices would be down
by the next day. A captain doubted this,
and so Elisha prophesied that he
would see this happen, though he would not eat
the food for sale. Some lepers went to see
the camp of Syria, and they found it empty.
They stole some gold and silver, then they went
to tell the king of Israel, who thought that now
his enemies were going to ambush him.
He sent some men to spy the land, and they
returned to say the Syrians had departed
because they thought they'd heard a huge
army approaching. Then the price of food
plummeted, now the siege was over, but
the captain who had disbelieved the word
about the prices, which Elisha had
spoken, was trodden in the rushing crowd,
and died, so did not eat the food for sale.

VI

ELISHA brought about events of moment
in Syria and in Israel. He ensured
that Hazael would become the next king
of Syria, and Hazael rose up
against his king and took control. Likewise,
in Israel, Jehu mutinied because
Elisha sent a messenger to take
a flask of oil, anointing him as king.
Jehu then slaughtered all the prophets

loyal to Baal and Jezebel, who was
killed at his word. Next he destroyed the temple
of Baal and made it a latrine. Yet still,
Jehu infringed the Lord's commandments, though
his power and might became proverbial.
But Hazael, the king of Syria, fought hard
against the Israelites in Jehu's time
and afterwards. He conquered Gath, but not
Jerusalem, whose people gave him gifts.

VII

ELISHA had become so ill, he knew
that he must die, so Joash king of Israel,
went down to him and grieved at this sad news.
Elisha told the king to take a bow
and arrows and to shoot an arrow from
the window eastwards. Joash did as he
was asked, and then Elisha said, *Behold
the arrow of the Lord. This is a sign
of victory against the Syrians.*
Elisha then told Joash that he should
take all the arrows and should strike the ground
with them. So the king struck the ground three times.
At that Elisha said, *You should have struck
the ground five times at least. Now you will have
but three victories over Syria.*
The prophet thus was able to perform
prophetic actions even in his last
moments on earth. And then he died, his name
written for ever in the scroll of God.

AMOS
THE PROPHET

I

AMOS OF TEKOA in Judah was
a shepherd and in season he dressed fruit
on sycamore fig trees. But the Lord called
Amos to be his prophet and he went
north into Israel, there to preach God's word.
This was during the reigns of Jeroboam,
the king of Israel, and Uzziah king
of Judah, and two years before the well
remembered earthquake. Amos knew he had
his calling from the Lord himself, as if
God had arranged a meeting with him. He
had little choice in his vocation, for
he was aware that God entrusted him
with secrets hidden in the years to come.
Especially he knew that all his people
whom God had chosen, were to be chastised.

II

AMOS condemned the cruelty of men
in countries all around his native land,
but also spoke against the Israelites.
He said of Judah that they had infringed
the laws of God by straying from the paths
of truth. In Israel, too, he spoke against
their wicked ways, especially of those
who cheated the afflicted and the poor.
He censured their corruption and their gross
injustice, which they perpetrated, even
while they attended worship in God's house.
Reminding them of how their God had saved
their ancestors so many times, he warned
them of God's punishment to come. He told
the pampered women that they would be dragged

away like cattle and he prophesied
that wealthy wine bibbers, who lay on beds
of ivory, would soon be lost in exile,
that all their riches would be gone, that war
would bring defeat, disgrace and death.

III

AMOS told the people that the Lord
had given many warnings. Famine, drought
and swarms of locusts, and foul plague, should have
alerted them to God's displeasure. But
the people wandered far away from God
and would not turn again to him. He said
they should prepare to meet their God and warned
them of the coming judgement day. He said,
Seek good, not evil, for that Day will be
darkness, not light, arriving suddenly
as if you were at home, relaxing there
when a snake bit you. God says, " I despise
 your feasts and festivals; I hate the sound
of instruments you play in your false worship;
and all the offerings you bring are useless.
Let justice flow like rushing waters: let
your righteousness be like a stream that springs
eternally. Thus Amos spoke God's word.

IV

AMOS saw God's power in the universe:
the One who forms the mountains and creates
the wind, reveals to man his thoughts, who makes
the morning darkness, and strides on the peaks
of the wide earth – the Lord, the God of hosts,
that is his name. The one who made Orion
and Pleiades, and changes darkness through
to dawning, then turns daytime into night;
who charges seas and oceans, spreading them

over the world – the Lord, that is his name.
The Lord, the God of hosts, the One who touches
the earth and it moves, rising like the Nile
and sinking down again, and making those
who live there mourn; the One who builds his rooms
in heaven and sets his vaults above the earth;
the One who summons water, pouring it
across the earth – the Lord, that is his name.

V

NOW IN THE TIME OF AMOS, Amaziah
was the chief priest in Bethel. He complained
to Jeroboam, king of Israel, that
Amos the prophet had denounced the king
and prophesied his death, as well as saying
that Israel would be exiled from his land.
Then Amaziah met the prophet, saying,
Go far from here, back to the land of Judah,
and eat and prophesy in Judah. Go,
do not return to Bethel, for it is
the sanctuary of the king. Then Amos
replied and said, *I am no prophet paid*
by man, but God has called me from my trade
to speak his word. So hear the word of God:
your wife shall be a city prostitute;
your children will be slain; and all your land
will be divided by your enemies;
and you yourself shall die in exile far
from here; and so with Israel's mighty men.

VI

THE LORD showed to Amos visions of judgement
and doom for Israel, but he prayed that these
might be averted. First he saw a plague
of locusts eating all the grass in Israel.
He asked the Lord to stop the plague

from coming, so the Lord agreed to this.
Next Amos saw a fire which ate up all
the land and sea. Again he asked the Lord
not to be harsh, and so the Lord agreed.
Next, Amos saw a plumb line hanging down
beside a wall which showed that Israel was
not straight; and then the Lord God vowed
that Israel would be desolate. The Lord
then showed to Amos summer fruit which would
go rotten; and the Lord said the end[8] was near,
and that the temple would be silent for
the sins of wealthy Israelites were many.
Then once again, the prophet had a vision;
he saw the Lord standing by the altar;
and God's word was that all the building would
be shattered, and survivors would be slain.
There would be no escape in heaven or earth,
or even in the depths of Sheol. These
were visions from the Lord as seen by Amos.

VII

Amos at last envisaged David's house[9]
rising again, after catastrophe.
He prophesied a future time when all
the hills of Israel would be sweet with wine;
when fertile land would sustain heavy crops;
when the lost fortunes of God's people would
be restored. They would rebuild their ruined towns
and plant their vineyards and their gardens. Like
the plants the people would be settled on
the land, the land given to them by God.
All this would happen on a very special day,
a day of happiness and joy for all.

HOSEA
THE PROPHET

I

IN THE LAST YEARS OF ISRAEL[10] the Lord
spoke to Hosea and instructed him
to marry a faithless woman who had been
a harlot. She produced three children who
received symbolic names. The first was called
Jezreel, a place of massacre in Israel,
and this sign meant that Israel's fate was sealed.
The second child was called Not-pitied, meaning
that God's pity for Israel was withdrawn.
The third child's name was Not-my-people, for
God had deserted them because of their
iniquity. Yet even so, in times
to come the nation would be one again,
for God's forgiveness would be sown once more.
Hosea kept his wife at home and would
not let her go with other men, and this
was Israel's need – to stay with God and stop
pursuing other imaginary gods.

II

NOW ISRAEL is a faithless wife for she
has played the harlot with her lovers, gods
whom she believes will give her daily bread
and flax and oil, providing all her needs.
But it is God who gives her all these things,
and yet she does not know it. But the Lord,
her faithful husband, will remove her grain
and wool and wine, and make an end of all
her merry festivals. Her jewellery
and rings will be her pride no longer, and her
adultery with Baal will be undone.
But I, the Lord, will court her once again,
and I shall be her husband, not her Baal;[11]

〈 91 〉

I will betroth her to myself and make
a covenant with her in steadfast love.
Then peace and righteousness and justice will
prevail, and I shall be your God, and you
shall be my people, prosperous in faith.

III

THE LORD disputes with Israel, for they have
not kept the law; there is no righteousness
in all the land and people do not know
the Lord. Prophets and priests are much to blame,
for they have disregarded what I have
revealed, and they are soaked in shame and sin.
I will repay them for their deeds. The whole
nation has played the harlot with their idols;
they offer sacrifices on high hills,
and under shady trees, to images
of wood; and then the men consort
with temple prostitutes – but they shall fall
in ruins. Israel will look for their God,
but he will hide himself from them, for they
are faithless. But alarms will sound across
the valleys when God's day of punishment
arrives. They will be carried away and torn
apart, as lions tear apart their prey.

IV

ISRAEL returned to me for a short time,
repenting of their guilty ways, but then
they sinned again. Their love for me is like
a morning cloud, or dew that soon dries up.
Their sacrifices are in vain unless they show
me steadfast love. I wish to heal my people,
but evil deeds abound among them, for
even the royal house is filled with acts
of wickedness; but I will soon chastise

them for their lies and treachery. I would
redeem them from their sins, but they turn again
to Baal. A warning trumpet sounds, for they
have sealed their own destruction. They sow
a wind, but they shall reap a whirlwind which
will sweep them all away. They have forgotten
that I the Lord am their Creator, but
fire shall consume them. They shall not remain
in this, my land; they shall be taken far
from here, to Egypt and Assyria.
Their festivals will end, their worship will
be lost. They drive the prophet mad and men
of spirit are made fools by their offences.

V

WHEN ISRAEL was young I called him out
of Egypt; as my son I summoned him
with love; sadly, the more I called, the more
he went away from me. I taught him how
to walk and held him in my arms; I gave
him food and led him with my love. But no,
he would not follow where I wished to guide him.
Some will return to Egypt, and some
will find Assyria is their king. Their towns
and fortresses will be destroyed, but yet
I love them and my heart is sore. How can
I give my children up? I spoke to them
through many prophets, gave them visions, yet
still they ignore my word. They make false gods
of silver, crafted carefully; but I
shall scatter them like chaff before the wind.
I am the Lord, your God: there is no god
but me. I am your saviour, and there is
no other way to save your souls from death.

VI

RETURN, O Israel, to the Lord your God:
repent and ask forgiveness from the Lord.
For I will heal their faithlessness, and I
will love them without bar, for I am now
turning away from anger, and I shall
be like dew upon the lily. Israel shall
be as a poplar tree, shoots spreading out;
in my eyes they shall be as beautiful
as any olive tree and scented like
the vales of Lebanon. Prosperity
shall rest upon them, and they shall be as
the wine from many vineyards. I am he
who cares for you, not senseless idols. My
pathways are straight and upright men shall walk
under my shade, protected from all evil.

ISAIAH
OF JERUSALEM[12]

I

ISAIAH HEARD God's call in the same year
that King Uzziah died. The prophet said,
There I was in the temple, when I saw
a vision of the Lord enthroned on high.
The six winged seraphim hovered above,
calling to one another:
'HOLY, HOLY, IS THE LORD OF HOSTS;
THE WHOLE EARTH IS FULL OF HIS GLORY.'
The temple filled with smoke and all the walls
shook with the shock as God's voice called to me.
I felt unclean before this holiness, but one
seraph took in his hand a burning coal
and touched my lips, thus cleansing me, a sign
that God had purged my guilt. God spoke and said,
Whom shall I send and who will go for us?
Trembling, I said, *Here I am, Lord, send me.*

Then the Lord said, *Go to your people who do*
not understand my word, and say to them
that I shall be their judge, that their whole land
will become desolate like a burnt oak,
though my holy seed will grow from the stump.

II

YOUR SACRIFICES and burnt offerings
are nothing to the Lord, who says, *Your feasts*
and festivals are wearisome, for I
require good, not evil, justice not
oppression. I once planted vines and cared
for them, but wild grapes grew, so now I shall
destroy my vineyard, house of Israel, Judah
my chosen people. Now the haughty shall
be humbled, and the Lord's day will come soon,
that day when God will be exalted, when
the terror of the Lord destroys all idols,
when wanton women will be stripped of jewels.
Woeful shall be the day when wickedness
is punished, so woeful that day, for strong
enemies will destroy this land. But yet,
Jerusalem will be a centre for
all nations, and the laws of Zion will
prevail. God will be judge and peace will reign
and wars will end throughout the world. All swords
will then be changed to plough shares and all spears
will act as pruning hooks in God's new world.

III

SYRIA AND EPHRAIM threatened Judah, but
Isaiah the prophet told the king that this
plot would be foiled. He met king Ahaz
beside a pool and gave to him a sign
from God, about a royal son whose name
would be Immanuel,[13] born of a young

woman. Isaiah took his son to meet the king,
and the boy's name was Shearjashub.[14] Later
Isaiah had another son whose name
was Maher-shalal-hash-baz,[15] a sign
that soon Assyria would prevail against
the enemies of Judah. Isaiah warned
the king to place his trust in God, and not
to have faith in Assyrian power. *For now,*
Isaiah said, *the Lord allows the rod*
of cruel Assyrian might to be his tool,
but soon the Holy One of Israel will
destroy Assyria with His potent fire.

IV

A BRILLIANT LIGHT has broken upon those
who walked in darkest gloom, for now the rod
of tyranny is broken and the nation
rejoices at the day of victory.
A child is born, a son has come, and he
shall sit on David's throne; and he shall be
called Wonderful, Counsellor, Omnipotent,
Eternal Father and the Prince of Peace.
He shall uphold the cause of right and, through
the zeal of God, shall rule in equity.
God's Spirit shall be his, wisdom and might,
knowledge and understanding; and fear of God
shall be his sure delight. He shall espouse
the cause of poor and needy citizens,
and he shall smite the wicked with his rod.
A time of peace shall come, when wolf and lamb,
leopard and kid, lion and calf, and bear
and cow – shall live together. A young child
shall lead them, and the earth shall be as full
of godly knowledge as the waters flood
the sea. Then, Jesse's root shall be an ensign
for all the scattered peoples of the world.

V

THE DAY OF THE LORD will descend upon
the hosts of Babylon, and their false pride
will be brought low. Their king, who thought himself
a god, will fall into the pit of death.
Assyria will be broken and all Moab
will be overrun. Philistia
will fade, Damscus lie in ruins, and there
in Ethopia the birds of prey
will eat their fill. A civil war will rise
in Egypt, and the Nile will become dry;
but then they will worship God, for He
will soon deliver them. And in that day
Assyria and Egypt will be one
with Israel, and their many peoples blessed.
Before that day, even Jerusalem
will weep with bitter tears, and Tyre will
come to naught along with Sidon's sons.
Yet through all this, the Lord will dwell in Zion,
for there the Lord of hosts upholds his name.

VI

THE LORD SAYS, *See! In Zion I shall lay*
a tested stone, a cornerstone; believe
but do not hurry past. Justice shall be
the line and righteousness the weight by which
my people's actions shall be judged. Hear this!
People draw near with words, but their hearts
are far away from me, for they learn reverence
by rote; but I shall turn their hearts again,
and they shall fear the Holy One of Jacob.
The Lord is waiting to be gracious for
he is a God of mercy and of justice. Those
who wait upon his word shall have his blessing.
Though you may know adversity, the Lord
himself shall teach you which pathway to take.
Rely upon the Lord, and not upon

the power of Egypt, and you will receive
good harvests and have many cattle, for
the Lord will walk with you. Even the moon
above your heads will shine more brightly than
the sun; and every day the sun will shine
like seven days, for God will heal your wounds.
The Lord will spare Jerusalem – will
protect his city from Assyrian foes.
The Lord, he is our King, right here in Zion,
and insolent invaders will be expelled.

VII

THE DESERT and the wilderness will bloom
with flowers, and the majesty and beauty
of Lebanon and Carmel will be there.
The glory of the Lord will then be seen
and God will come to save his fearful people.
The blind shall see, the deaf shall hear, the lame
shall walk and then the dumb of tongue shall sing.
Pools of fresh water shall appear, and springs
and streams shall flow abundantly. A road
shall run, a Holy Way through a wilderness,
and only the redeemed shall walk along
the highway as they sing their way to Zion.
Gladness and joy shall fill their hearts and all
their sighs of sorrow shall then fly away.

VIII

THE SON OF AHAZ, Hezekiah, faced
Assyrian might led by Sennacherib.
The king was much afraid and sent some men
to ask Isaiah what to do. The prophet said
that the Assyrian king would never take
Jerusalem. Yet more threats came to fret
King Hezekiah; so the king prayed long
and earnestly, asking the Lord for help.

Isaiah sent to Hezekiah and he said,
Thus says the Lord: *I shall answer your prayer:*
Assyrian soldiers shall not take the town.
And soon Isaiah's prophecy came true,
for in Assyria's camp many men died
during the night. Sennacherib drew back
and marched to Nineveh, and there his sons
assassinated him. But Hezekiah
fell ill and prayed to God for help. Isaiah
approached the king and said, *Your prayer*
is answered. God will grant a sign for you.
The sun's shadow will go backwards ten steps
on the sun dial of Ahaz. The king was cured
of sickness by Isaiah. Around that time
the king of Babylon sent messengers
with gifts and Hezekiah showed them all
his treasures. But Isaiah prophesied
that in the future all these treasures would
be carried off as spoil to Babylon.

THE UNKNOWN
ISAIAH[16]

I

MAKE READY the Lord's way across the desert,
for God will make the pathway level. Then
the glory of the Lord will be revealed to all,
for God has spoken. "B*ut what shall I say?*"
The answer came, *The world and people are*
of short duration, but the word of God
will still remain. "*What is your word, O Lord?*"
Jerusalem will be a herald bringing
good news. Zion will say to Judah, 'God
is coming like a shepherd holding lambs,
and he will feed his flock with love and care.'

II

WHO CAN MEASURE all earth and heaven but God?
Who can advise the Lord or teach his Spirit?
The nations of the world are dust to him,
and all the peoples like a drop of water.
How can he be compared to statues made
of wood and metal, formed by human hands?
He is the Holy One, beyond compare,
the everlasting God who made the world.
Those who have faith will stand before him.
I am the Lord, first and last: I am he.
I am the Lord, and I have called you forth
and made a lasting covenant with you.
I am the Lord: there is no other god,
and I shall save my people. Every knee
shall bow to me and every tongue confess
my name. I comfort you, and hold you safe
under the shadow of my mighty hand.

III

THE PUNISHMENT of Israel is complete
for now the Lord will comfort all his people.
But haughty nations will receive harsh judgement:
they are deluded and their gods are false.
Jacob, be strong and do not fear, for I
the Lord your God have called your name.
I will protect you from all harm, from fire
and flood, because I am your Saviour, I
who formed you as my chosen people.
I, your Redeemer, will shatter the bars
of Babylon where gods are cheaply made.
But you, O Israel, will be saved, renewed,
for I, the Lord, will now blot out your sins.
My shepherd and anointed one is Cyrus,
and he will be my instrument to free
my people from their bondage and to send
them to their home, for Babylon will fall.

I have refined you, Israel: suffering
has brought you back to me. Now you will hear
a new and hidden thing in what I do,
a deed which all the nations will behold,
when I send you from Babylon across
the desert wastes, your hearts replete with joy.
The Lord has comforted his people; from
their darkened prison they shall be released.
As once I made a pathway through the sea
to save their fathers, so I save my people
yet again. They shall return to Zion, glad
of heart, and sorrow will be far from them.

IV

YOU ARE MY SERVANT, Israel, and I will help
you when your enemies are all around.
You are my choice, and I delight in you;
my Spirit is upon you and the nations
will know that justice is their lot through you.
Your faithfulness will hold you to your task,
and no complaint will echo in the street.
God named you in the womb and made you like
a sword or shiny arrow in his hand.
You will restore the scattered tribes of Israel
and your light will reach out across the world.
Each morning God will waken you and speak
his word, but you will be humiliated
and spit upon. Remember that I shall
stand up with you and prove your innocence.

V

ALTHOUGH MY SERVANT is not fair to look
upon, nations and kings will be amazed.
He was despised, forsaken, sorrowful,
and full of grief; and he has carried our
grief and misfortune. For us he was bruised

and punished, and by his hurt we are healed;
we have strayed far from God, but he has borne
our sins upon his shoulders. Like a lamb
led dumbly and unjustly to the slaughter,
he died for our transgressions. He was good,
and not a man of violence, but he
went to the grave of a rich man. It was
by God's will that he was afflicted when
he offered himself, pouring out his soul
to death. But even so, he will be great,
and he shall see prosperity. He will
behold his offspring and his spirit will
be satisfied with the fruit of his toil.

VI

THE LORD has not forsaken you, O Zion,
and you will overcome your enemies.
Your ruins will be raised again and she
who was bereaved and barren will be blessed
with countless children. Soon my signal will
be seen afar and all your sons and daughters
will come to you; and kings and queens will bow
before you; for I am your Saviour, your
Redeemer, and my power is all consuming.
Jerusalem was drunk and staggering
after my cup of wrath was given to her.
But now she must stand up, for I, the Lord,
will comfort her and plead her cause. Awake!
O Zion, and put on your festal garments;
your bonds will now be loosed and shaken off.
I will redeem you and my name will be
upon your lips. Good news is brought by one
who publishes salvation: now God reigns
and watchmen on your towers have seen the Lord
returning to Jerusalem. O sing
aloud, you ruined city, for the Lord
has bared his holy arm before the eyes
of many nations. Do not go in haste,

nor run in fear, for I the Lord will go
before you and behind you for your safety.

VII

ENLARGE YOUR TENT, O barren one, for
your children will be many and your seeds
will spread abroad. Forget your shame, for I,
your husband, will redeem you. It was but
for a short time that I forsook you, hid
my face from you, but now compassion moves
my heart, and you will know my love. Just as
I promised Noah, so shall I promise you:
my steadfast love, my peaceful covenant,
shall never be removed. Storms have beset
your walls, but I will make you now a city
founded on sapphires and all glittering
with precious stones. Prosperity will be
your heritage and righteousness your strength.
Your vindication is from me, the Lord,
and you shall conquer any who dispute
with you; and enemies will fall before you.

VIII

COME NOW TO ME, my people, if you thirst,
or if you hunger: eat and drink without
a price. Hear, that your soul may live, and I
will make a covenant of constant love
with you. You will be glorified among
the nations, for your God, the Holy One
of Israel, will exalt you; just as David
was once a witness to the peoples. Seek
the Lord, for he is near to you: return
to him for pardon. I am far beyond
your thoughts and ways; for never shall my word
return to me without accomplishing
my purpose. Peace and joy will be your lot,

and your sign from me will grow upon
the spreading cypress and the myrtle branch.

JEREMIAH
THE PROPHET

I

GOD'S WORD first came to me during the reign
of king Josiah – and from then till Judah
fell to the Babylonians. I felt
I was too young to be a prophet, but
the Lord promised to be with me, and touched
my mouth to speak his word. He spoke to me
through signs and told me he was watching over
his word, that evil would descend upon
the land from northern tribes. Also the Lord
told me that, though enemies would beset me,
he would defend me and would make me strong
to stand against them. But God's word was fearful,
and I could see destruction all around.
Mountains were quaking and the sky was black;
the whole earth was an empty waste, and life
was gone. I heard the cry of Zion's daughter,
and saw her stretching out her hands in grief.

II

JUDAH AND ISRAEL, you departed from
my ways. I planted you, a fruitful vine,
but you became wild and unfruitful. You
worshipped dead stones and mindless trees, but where
are your false gods? You are two faithless sisters,
but now you must return to me. A strong
enemy will conquer you; his chariots
are swift, a whirlwind blowing you away.
Prophet and priest are false, and so your city,
Zion, will fall: be warned Jerusalem!

Injustice rules: my laws are cast aside.
Truth is ignored: oppression is widespread.
Jerusalem will be a ruin, and all
of Judah desolate – thus says the Lord.
I am the Lord: my steadfast love is endless,
and righteousness and justice are my joy.

III

YOU STAND BEFORE ME in my temple where
you seek salvation, but you break my laws
and worship falsely. Here your prayers will not
be heeded, and I shall destroy this house.
Because you have not kept my word, these streets
will soon be silent and your land a waste.
Your name is great, O Lord, and you are King
of all the nations, the true God, the living God.
You are Creator and your wisdom set
the earth in place, and all the powers that move
in nature speak your word. There is no breath
or spirit in the crafted images
made by men's hands. Men have deserted God
and he is wounded at his loss; for all
the flock is scattered far and wide and they
have broken his explicit covenant.
Trust not in men, but put your trust in God
and you will harvest many blessings; but
remember, God will search your heart and mind
and you will gain your just deserts. Our God
is Israel's hope: heal me O Lord, and I
shall soon be healed. I praise you, Lord, my God.

IV

LIKE A LAMB LED TO SLAUGHTER, I was not
aware that they were hatching plots against
me, Jeremiah, planning to despatch
my soul. I plead my case with you, O Lord:

vengeance is yours. The wicked seem to prosper,
but I have faith in God who knows my heart.
But the Lord told me that worse was to come.
I rue the day that I was born: I have
followed the good; I have avoided men
to sit alone, because God called me – yet
my pain is never ending. Lord, you have
deceived me like a stream that fails! But God
was adamant. I had no choice: I had
to prophesy. His promise was to make
me hard against my enemies, to save
my life. But they have dug a pit to trap
me, so I curse their families, O Lord.
May they be overthrown by your great might!
May your wrath fall upon them, as you will!

V

Now Jeremiah preached God's word in parables.
The prophet saw a potter making pots
and one was spoiled; but the used clay was worked
again, and Jeremiah saw that God
would do the same with all his people if
they did not turn to him in righteousness.
Then Jeremiah saw an iron pen
which had a diamond point and he realised
that Judah's sins were written with that pen
upon the tablet of their faithless heart.
The prophet took a waist cloth and he hid
it in a cleft of rock upon the bank
of the Euphrates. When he came to pick
it up, the cloth was spoiled. So would it be
with Judah who clung to their God much as
the waist cloth. They would now be useless, for
their stubborn ways had turned them far from God.
Then Jeremiah took a flask of pot
and in the Hinnom valley, witnessed by
some priests, shattered the flask. So would the Lord
do to his people and their towns because

their faithless hearts had turned away from God
Later, in Babylon, where many men
were exiled from their promised land, the Lord
showed Jeremiah some fresh figs and some
which had gone bad. The good figs were the exiles
who would return wholeheartedly to God:
the bad figs were the king and princes who
would be destroyed because their sin was great.

VI

KING ZEDEKIAH sent some men to ask
the word of God from Jeremiah, for
he was concerned about the danger posed
by Nebuchrezzar, king of Babylon.
But Jeremiah told the messengers
that Babylon would have the victory.
Then Jeremiah went to see the king
and warned him that injustices and wrongs
against the poor and fatherless, the alien
and widow, would be punished by the Lord.
He also told the king that all his house
would fall because God's covenant had been
forsaken; and that his great city would be made
desolate. Jeremiah spoke to all
the people of Jerusalem and Judah:
For twenty three years of my life I have
preached God's word here, but you have not heeded
what I have said. Turn from your evil ways
and God may yet forgive your sins. But no,
you will not listen, and your fate is sealed.
The Babylonians will overrun
your land and make you slaves in Babylon.

VII

SOME PRINCES, priests and prophets wished to kill
the prophet Jeremiah for preaching treason

in the Lord's name. But others disagreed.
He had already been humiliated
in the stocks – yet he preached on, and one day
strapped round his neck a yoke to show that Judah
and other nations would be servants, forced
by Babylon to serve their king. He mocked
those prophets who denied his word. One such,
a man called Hananiah said the Lord
would break the yoke of Babylon. This man
took hold of Jeremiah's yoke and broke it.
But Jeremiah spoke again to say
the yoke of Babylon was barred with iron.
The prophet wrote to those who had gone
earlier to Babylon, advising them
to put down roots, because seventy years
would be their time in Babylon.

VIII

THE KING[17] imprisoned Jeremiah for
his prophecies of doom on Judah, but
the prophet would not change his stance; however,
the prophet bought a field and stored the deeds
to show that after exile people would
have property again. The Lord revealed
also that in the future David's son
would reign once more. But first, calamity
must come, and Babylon would take the king
of Judah into Babylon. The prophet praised
the Rechabites[18] for their staunch discipline
and held them up as an example for
all other men of Judah. Then the prophet
wrote on a scroll God's word of judgement. This
his scribe read to the people, but the king
destroyed the scroll. But even so, the king
consulted Jeremiah while he was
in prison. But then, Jeremiah was
thrown down a well and left to die because
because he prophesied disaster for

his people. Yet the king gave leave for him
to be brought up from there, and wished to ask
the prophet's counsel, but refused to listen.
Too soon the city fell, and so the king
was caught and had his eyes put out by king
Nebuchadrezzar, though the prophet was
in favour with the Babylonians.
A remnant stayed in Judah, ruled by a man
called Gedeliah, who unhappily was slain
in a rebellion. Jeremiah went
to Egypt, there to join a Jewish remnant;
but he foretold that Babylon would take
the land of Egypt. Some exiles in Egypt
worshipped Egyptian gods, and Jeremiah
warned them of punishment for all their sins.

IX

A DAY OF VENGEANCE came against the land
of Egypt, as the prophet had foretold:
the Babylonians had victory
over Pharaoh their king. Philistia
and Moab will conquered by their foes;
and Edom and Damascus will be ruined;
as will Kedar and Elam fall. But
even the Babylonians will find
defeat, and their proud city will be
destroyed, because the Lord is fierce against
them, the Lord God who loves Jerusalem

X

THE LORD told Jeremiah that he must
write down a long term prophecy. *Your land
will be restored, O Israel, and your songs
will echo through the streets, for I shall be
your God and you shall be my people. Health
will come to you and I shall heal your wounds.*

My everlasting love will be with you
and you will plant your vineyards and go up
to Zion for your festivals. I will
transform your mourning into joy and I
will comfort you. Rachel will weep no longer
for her offspring: her children will return
to her. My heart yearns for my son and I
shall have mercy on him. My daughter has
been faithless, but I shall restore her. Then
I shall make a new covenant with all
my people: for my law will be inscribed
upon their hearts. They will not need a teacher,
for they will all know me. I shall forgive
their past iniquity, and all their sins
will be forgotten. As the sun and moon
and stars are set in place, so shall my people
always be mine, a nation in my care.

EZEKIEL
THE PROPHET

I

EXILED IN BABYLON, I felt the hand
of God upon me, and visions came to me.
I saw four strange creatures emerge from out
of a huge cloud; bright fire and lightning shot
from their midst as they darted to and fro;
each had four faces, one man-like, one like
an ox, another like a lion, while
he fourth was like an eagle. Then I saw
beside them four wheels within wheels, with eyes
around their rims, all driven by their spirits.
Over them hung a dome of sky, all bright
like crystal. Their wings whirred like thunder from
God himself. Above the dome I saw a throne
glittering with sapphire stones, on which there sat
a fiery human shape surrounded by
the brightness of a rainbow. This was like

the glory of the Lord, and I bowed down
and listened to the voice which spoke to me.

II

THE VOICE SAID TO ME, *Son of man, do this:*
go to my people Israel who have turned
away from me, and speak my words. I saw
a scroll on which were words of woe. I ate
the scroll and it was sweet. The voice of God
instructed me to speak to them despite
the stubbornness of all their hearts.
The Spirit took me then and lifted me
to be among the exiles, and I heard
the thunder of his whirring wheels and wings.
For seven days I was in shock, and then
the Lord instructed me to be a watchman,
and to denounce the sinner in his plight,
appealing for repentance. Then the Lord
carried me down into the valley where
I saw his glory once again. He told
me that I must go home, there to be bound
like all the exiles; and to be dumb – until
the Lord unloosed my tongue. But I knew well
that no-one would take heed of what I said.

III

THROUGH MANY SIGNS AND PROPHECIES I told
them of the ruin of Jerusalem,
and of their hapless life in exile. *God's*
judgement will come because of your delight
in your false worship. All the land will be
a desolation and your dead will lie
around your altars. Others will be dragged
and driven far away to exile. Yes,
your doom is sealed: your pride will fall in shame.
Silver and gold will never save you from

your just deserts. The Spirit lifted me
and took me to Jerusalem and there
I saw the glory of the Lord among
their vile abominations. Then I knew
that only those bearing God's mark would be
preserved and saved. I saw another vision
of God's glory, surrounded by the wings
of cherubim and shining, whirring wheels.
The Spirit told me there that in the future
Israel would be restored, their stony hearts
renewed as flesh, that He would be their God
and they would be his chosen, faithful people.

IV

THROUGH SIGNS I spoke again about the exile
and emphasised that this would happen soon.
To those who prophesied that peace would reign
I said that God would smite them for their lies.
Even if Noah, Job and Daniel lived
within the city, yet it would be ruined
except for them alone. God will send out
four painful judgements on the land: the sword,
a famine, pestilence and raging beasts.
Jerusalem is like a vine which bears
no fruit; God found you, nurtured you and gave
you wealth and splendour, but ingratitude
was your reward. You acted as a harlot,
betraying God's trust. Corruption is
your path, and bribery your living – so
you have become as dross to melt away.

V

THE KING OF BABYLON swooped down, just like
an eagle which plucks off a cedar branch,
to take the king of Judah far away.
Then Babylon set up another king

to rule in Judah, like a spreading vine,
but that vine will wither away, because
that vine of Judah bent its roots towards
the power of Egypt, an eagle plumed
with bright feathers. Judah has broken trust
with Babylon and will die. But the Lord
will take a cedar branch and plant it high
upon the mount of Israel and it will
become a noble tree. This is God's word.

VI

TWO SISTERS took to harlotry though they
were God's possession and his loves. One was
Samaria,[19] and she gave up her virtue
to the Assyrians who destroyed her land.
The other was Jerusalem[20] who made
herself a harlot with Assyria,
and then turned to the Babylonians
to satisfy her lewdness. But she will
be slaughtered by her lovers, and will go
the same way as her sister. Like a pot
set on to boil, the fire burning all
around, the flesh and bones seething hot –
so will Judah be, for flesh and bone will fall
into the fire. Even the copper pot
will melt and be destroyed. So will it be
with Judah for her many sins; and then
the sanctuary of their God will be
defiled and all Jerusalem be ruined.
Yet even now, the wicked man who turns
away from sin will surely live; but always
remember that each man must take the load
of his own sin. A son will not be punished
for what his father has done wrong, nor will
a father be chastised for his son's sins.

VII

AMMON showed joy at Israel's loss and they
shall suffer for their sins and be destroyed;
so shall it be with Moab and with Edom,
for they despised the people of my choice;
likewise Philistia shall be cut off.
The arrogance of Tyre shall be brought low
when Babylon shall trample through their streets
and Tyrians shall meet a dreadful end.
The wealth of Tyre shall be taken in war
and their lament shall echo on the seas.
The prince of Tyre believes he is a god,
but though he is a man of wealth, his fall
from grace is sure; from Eden he shall be
cast out and all his precious stones shall be
taken away by the cherub set to guard
God's holy mountain from all evil. His
perfection shall be marred and he shall be
consumed by holy, cleansing fire.
Pharaoh of Egypt shall be hooked, as fish
are hooked beside the Nile, and Egypt shall
be desolate and all their idols shall
be dross. His people shall be scattered far
and wide, his army slain, his body laid
in shame among unholy multitudes.

VIII

JERUSALEM has fallen, and the Lord
has said to me: *O son of man, you must
alert the shepherds like a watchman. Tell
the shepherds of my people that I am
against them and their shepherding. I shall
be shepherd to my people and I shall
seek my sheep out, to rescue them, to bring
them back to their own land where they shall prosper.*
The Lord will give a new heart to his people:
a new spirit will be theirs and their

stone hearts will be replaced with hearts of flesh.
The Lord will vindicate his holy name
and all his people will be cleansed of sin.
The valley of dry bones will know the breath
of life, and flesh will grow upon the bones;
the bones will come together, bone to bone,
as the whole house of Israel springs to life.
He will now raise his people from the grave
and they shall know that he is God and Lord.
Ephraim[21] and Judah shall be joined as one,
and David once again shall rule; and all
of them shall have one shepherd. God shall
renew his covenant of peace with Israel,
and he shall be their God and they his people.
Not even Gog[22] with all his powers will gain
the victory over God's people, Israel.

IX

THE LORD'S HAND was upon me and I saw
a vision of a city where a man
showed me the temple, measuring its walls
and all its courts. He showed me all the rooms
and took me to the holy place where he
measured its size. Along the nave were carved
palm trees and cherubim. There he showed me
the altar. Afterwards he measured all
the temple area. I stood beside
the gate and saw the glory of the Lord
enter and fill the temple. Then the Lord
told me about the priests and Levites who
would serve him there. I was then told of all
the festivals and services which would
take place within the temple. Water flowed
out of the door of this great temple, forming
a river which poured down into the desert
and made it fertile. Then the Lord explained
the bounds of Israel and the tribal portions.

HAGGAI
THE PROPHET

I

HAGGAI spoke God's word to all the remnant
of Judah, and to Joshua, the priest,
also to Zerubbabel governor
of Judah. *Harvests are not good because*
of drought. This is because you have not built
a house for me, the Lord your God. So then
the temple was begun and soon the prophet
said that the Lord was with them. Again
the word of God was given to Haggai:
Take courage, Zerubbabel and your priest,
Joshua. Judah will be splendid once
again. Riches will come to this your land.
But the whole nation is unclean and must
reform in holiness. Return to me,
my chosen ones, and you will have my blessing.
When nations shake at my command, then you,
Zerubbabel, my chosen leader, will
be like a signet ring before the world.

ZECHARIAH
THE PROPHET

I

THE WORLD is easy at this time, but now
the Lord of hosts is angry with the nations;
and he will favour Zion, though her sons
have sinned, both now and in past times. From now
Jerusalem will prosper and shall be
the chosen city of the Lord as once
it was. The city will be measured by
the angels, for its people will be many;
and now the glory of the Lord will dwell
within her. Satan accuses Joshua,

but God accuses Satan and will dress
his priest in fresh, clean clothes, provided that
he walks in righteous ways. An angel showed
me a golden lampstand and beside it stood
two olive trees, the chosen of the Lord.
For Zerubbabel will raise up and finish
this house of God which he has founded here.

II

ACCORDING to this flying scroll I see,
all thieves and liars shall be destroyed. The Lord's
horses and chariots will patrol the earth,
one chariot for each of the four winds.
God's word is this: take now silver and gold
and make a crown for Joshua the priest.
The Branch shall sit upon a throne and he
shall raise the temple of the Lord; from far
away people shall come to help to build.
Remember, people did not hear the Lord
and strayed from ways of righteousness; it was
then that the Lord scattered them in his wrath,
and so the land they left was desolate.
The Lord is jealous for Jerusalem: he will
return to Zion which shall be now named
the faithful city. Children will then play
along the streets and all the elderly
will sit in peace. The remnant will dwell here
in safety, clothed in righteousness; the land
will yield good fruit and blessings will be theirs.
Speak truth and avoid evil, that you may
take part in cheerful feasts of joy and gladness.
People from many places will come here
to ask the favour of the Lord, and they
will ask to go with Jewish people, for
the Lord is with them in their daily lives.

III [23]

NO MORE oppressors will invade God's city:
from Tyre to Askelon will be the Lord's domain.
Rejoice, O daughter of Jerusalem,
your king is coming, riding on an ass.
He is victorious and he will bring
his peaceful reign throughout the world. The blood
of the Lord's covenant is with you, Zion,
and your sons will defeat the sons of Greece.
The Lord will come in a whirlwind and will
be saviour to his people, jewels set
in a crown. Take no notice of false prophets,
for God himself will be your shepherd. Judah
will be his steed in battle, strengthened by
his presence. Soon his people will come back
and he will gather them, for he is their
Redeemer. They will be strong in the Lord.

IV

AT THE LORD'S WORD I took two staffs, one for Grace
and one for Union. I broke the first
of the two staffs, which signified that God's
grace was now void, his covenant annulled.
I broke the second staff which signified
that Judah was no longer Israel's brother.
Yet, on the set day of the Lord, all nations
which strike Jerusalem shall be destroyed.
Then shall they mourn the one they pierced, and God's
compassion shall be theirs. Bathed in a fountain,
all shall be cleansed of sin; and prophets shall
be shamed and wounded by their friends and parents.
After destruction then the Lord will come;
and day shall light the darkness of the night;
and from Jerusalem, water of life
shall flow in summer as in wintertime.
The Lord shall rule the whole wide earth and so
the city of the Lord shall stand unbowed,

despite the warring nations. Those who live,
surviving war and pestilence, shall come
to worship in Jerusalem. From then,
the holiness of God shall touch the bells
of horses and the bowls for sacrifice.

EZRA
MAN OF GOD

I

CYRUS OF PERSIA conquered Babylon
and sent some Jewish people back to Judah,
there to rebuild Jerusalem and raise
a temple for the Lord. After some time
and many difficulties they rebuilt
the city and the temple. Ezra was
then sent from Babylon to help his people
with letters from a later Persian king.
Before departure Ezra prayed and kept
a fast with all his company. He brought
silver and gold as gifts for the Lord's temple.
Through many dangers they at last arrived
and gave their gifts to priests in the Lord's house.
They offered sacrifices in thanksgiving;
and Ezra handed over messages for
all the king's servants in the provinces.

II

NOW AT A LATER TIME, Ezra the priest
gathered the people in the square and read
the law of God to them. Then Ezra helped
the people to appreciate and know
the meaning of the law, helped in this task
by other teachers. Ezra blessed the people
and they replied *Amen!* That day was made
a festival. The following day the priests

and scribes and Levites studied under Ezra.
They learned that booths should be erected at
the festival of booths. So all the people
gathered the branches from the palm and olive,
and other trees to build their booths upon
the roofs of all their houses, and around
the temple courts. Ezra then prayed and told
the people of the history of Israel,
about God's grace and Israel's faithlessness.
At that, a covenant was made and sealed
by princes, priests and Levites under God.

NEHEMIAH
GREAT LEADER

I

LIVING IN SUSA,[24] Nehemiah heard
that in Jerusalem the walls and gates
had been destroyed. He wept and prayed. The king
whom Nehemiah served noticed his sadness,
and asked the reason. Nehemiah told
the king, who gave permission for a journey
to Jerusalem to help the people there.
So Nehemiah travelled to the city
with letters of authority. He viewed
the walls, then told the Jews to start rebuilding.
But enemies arose to hinder what
the Jews were striving to achieve, so guards
were set upon the walls. The men who laboured
also bore weapons as they worked. When all
seemed well the people started grumbling
because the nobles were extorting grain
and money. Nehemiah gathered all
the nobles and officials and berated them.
So all of them took vows to cease from their
corruption. Nehemiah was appointed
as governor of Judah but he did
not use his power foolishly, and cared

for all the people. Enemies again arose,
accusing Nehemiah of ambition
to be their king. They then made plots against
him, trying to besmirch his reputation.
At last the wall was finished with God's help,
and Nehemiah organised the temple
and all the city, with two men in charge,
one of them being his brother, Hanani.

II

IN TIME there was a joyful dedication
of the new walls, and people came from all
the villages around the city. The priests
and Levites purified the people. Then
there was a great procession on the wall,
and thanksgiving and sacrifices
in the great temple. Then the laws of Moses
were read to all the people. Nehemiah
went back to see the king in Babylon,
but yet again returned to set aright
corruption and injustices in Judah.
He also had to organise the rites
for worship in the temple once again.
People transgressed the Sabbath with their trade,
so Nehemiah closed the city gates
during the Sabbath. Furthermore he made
all marriages to foreigners unlawful.
And so it was that Nehemiah served
his God by bringing order to his people.

ESTHER
JEWISH QUEEN IN PERSIA

I

THE KING OF PERSIA was annoyed because
his wife was not compliant, so he put her aside

and chose another wife. His favour fell
on Esther, niece of Mordecai, a Jew
who lived in Susa.[25] So the Persian king,
Ahasuerus, set the crown upon
her head. There was a plot against the king,
and through her uncle, Esther saved the king,
but then her Jewish origin was known.
A man called Haman was promoted by
the king and this man hated Jews, especially
Mordecai, uncle of Esther, who
would not bow down to him. Now Haman plotted
against the Jews and said their laws were alien.
He turned the king against the Jewish race
and he decreed that every Jew should die.
But Mordecai ensured that Esther knew
about this evil plan. She then agreed
to go to see the king, if she was able,
to try to help her people. She required
of Mordecai that all the Jews should pray
 and fast, that God might help her in her task.

II

So ESTHER dressed in regal clothes and stood
opposite where the king's hall was. The king,
in passing, saw her and held out to her
the golden sceptre which allowed her access
to see the king. She asked the king to dinner,
along with Haman. Ahasuerus the king
promised Esther anything she asked, and she
invited them to come again the night
following. Haman boasted of this favour,
but planned to hang Mordecai, Esther's uncle,
next morning. But that night the king perused
the chronicles and found that Mordecai
had saved the king from death at some time past.
He called Haman and told the man to honour
Mordecai, which he did with hate and loathing.
Again the king and Haman dined with Esther

and Esther pleaded for her people's lives.
The king agreed and wished to know the name
of the man who had arranged it all. She then
denounced Haman, and he was hung instead
of Mordecai, who was promoted in
his place. Esther ensured that Jews in all
the provinces were safe from persecution,
and there was feasting and rejoicing. Since
that time, the Jews have kept the feast of Purim
to celebrate the time when Esther saved
her people from the evil plots of Haman.

JOB
A RIGHTEOUS MAN

I

JOB was a good and prosperous man who fell
upon bad times. He lost his fortune and was
covered with sores from head to foot. His faith
was tested by the power of Satan, but
he preserved himself from sin. Three old friends
arrived to comfort Job, who cursed the day
that he was born. The first friend[26] said to Job,
God is all powerful. Submit to his reproof.
He will deliver you from all your troubles.
Then Job replied, *Tell me where I have erred.*
What sins have I committed? Yet my life
is miserable. My life is but a breath
and now I wish to die." The second friend[27]
then said, *Our God will not reject a man*
who is free from all blame: but to forget
God is to fall. So pray, and turn to him
and he will come to you. Then Job replied,
This is so true, but who is righteous, face
to face with God? Yet I am innocent,
although I cannot answer him, for he
is our Creator. Time is fleeting but
my God is hiding from me. The third friend[28]

then spoke up, *How can you be pure? God will*
exact only what guilt deserves, or less.
Who can know God? Put wickedness away
from you and light will shine upon your life.
Then Job replied, *I am a laughing stock,*
but free from blame. I am as wise as you.
God is more powerful than earthly kings
and he controls the destiny of man.
Your words are fruitless but my cause is just.
In Sheol²⁹ I would hide from God until
his wrath is past, until my pain is gone.

II

JOB's first friend spoke again: *Your words are wind*
and touched with evil. Where is the fear of God?
Are you the only wise man? Defy God at your
own peril. Wealth will vanish when a man
is wicked. Job replied: *God has shown*
his hate for me, and I am broken, though
my prayers are pure. My friends despise my life
and I am full of grief, without a hope.
The second friend then spoke again: *You think*
us stupid, but your anger tears your soul
apart. The wicked have no light and they
will have no offspring. They are snared by sin.
Job said, *How long will you torment me with*
your words? You do me wrong. My glory is
all stripped away for no good reason. God
has laid his hand upon me; yet you pierce
my heart. I wish that all my words were written –
yet surely I know that my Redeemer lives.
The third friend then spoke up: *The pride*
of wicked men perishes on the dung heap.
Their greed will give no pleasure and their wealth
will be consumed. This is by God's decree.
Then Job replied: *Mock if you like, but hear*
my words. It is so true that wickedness
is subject to the wrath of God, but even

the wicked man is spared on that great day.
But what you say is false and vain and empty.

III

JOB's first friend spoke again: *Make God your treasure*
and not your gold. You think that God does not
perceive iniquity, but yet he does.
Repent and be at peace with God. Be humble,
and pray to God, and light will come to you.
Then Job replied: *Where can I find my God?*
Will he not heed my cries of grief? I have
kept to his word, but he stirs fear in me.
The wealthy prosper, yet God does not hear
the prayers of all the sick and dying. All
the powerful seem to have God's blessing, but
widows and needy órphans suffer pain.
Yet even mighty men are brought by God
to nothing. Then the second friend spoke up:
What man is righteous facing God? The sun
and moon are dark compared with Him. So how
can any son of man hope to be clean?
Job said, *God's sovereign power throughout the world*
is limitless. Though he has made my soul
bitter, I hold to my integrity.
The wicked reap their just deserts and meet
their doom. The mysteries of God's creation
baffle the wise, for wisdom has no price.
The wisdom of the Lord is fear of Him;
and understanding is departure from
all evil. I think back to prosperous days
when I could help my fellows – days long gone;
and now I am a fool to them, and all
my honour is blown away. My distress is keen.
I cry for help; but no help comes, though I
myself gave help to many. I repeat,
my heart is free from guilt. Let God reply –
for my just cause is surely known to him.

IV

ANOTHER MAN[30] came up to offer his
advice; and he was angry with the friends
of Job for failing him, and with Job too,
because he thought he was too proud to accept
his humble place before his God. He said to
Job's friends: *Your age does not give you a share*
of wisdom, for only God's breath in man
does that. And then he spoke to Job: *It is*
God's spirit which gives me the right to speak.
Now why do you contend against your God?
God speaks in many ways, and he is wrathful
when faced with wickedness. Repent and turn
to God and you will be redeemed. Job has
insisted he is innocent of wrong,
but God rewards or punishes according
to human deeds; and Job rebels against
the Lord in sinful pride. God watches over
the righteous: he is Almighty in his power.
Think of God's wondrous works; fear him and do
not dwell in your conceit, but rather fear God.

V

IN A WHIRLWIND God spoke to Job: *Where then*
were you when I created stars and oceans?
Can you produce a world with all its wonders,
or bring to birth the years and changing seasons?
The marvels of creation are untold and you
can only see a tiny part of all
that is. How can you argue with your God?
Then Job replied, *I am of no importance*
and my tongue is stilled for loss of words.
Then God went on: *I made you, just as I*
created mighty beasts that roam the land
and sport upon the seas. So will these beasts
make covenant with you? You tremble when
you see their face, and yet they are my creatures.

Then Job said: *I repent in dust and ashes*
for now I know your mighty power and wisdom,
and I perceive your will cannot be stayed.
Job's friends were called by God to make amends
for all their bad advice, but Job said prayers
for them, commending them to God. In time,
Job's fortunes were restored and he was blessed
with children and the heartfelt peace of God.

HABAKKUK
THE PROPHET

I

THE PROPHET cried to God for help because
wickedness and injustice were unbridled.
But God explained to Habakkuk that he
was raising armies from Chaldea which
would conquer many countries. At this news
the prophet understood that God was bringing
judgment and chastisement to wicked men.
The prophet watched for visions and he saw
that a wicked man would fail, though a man
of righteousness would live sustained by his
faithfulness.[31] Arrogance will lead to woe.
Woe to the man who plunders cruelly:
for he will in his turn be prey to plunder.
Woe to the man who gains by evil means:
for he will die as forfeit to his greed.
Woe to the man who builds on his iniquity:
for the Lord's glory will fill all the world.
Woe to the man who shows contempt for neighbours:
for all his glory will be drenched in shame.
Woe to the man who puts his trust in idols:
for God is watching in his holy temple.

II

O Lord, I fear your work, and pray your wrath
will be tempered with mercy, for you are
the Holy One surrounding heaven and earth.
He shook the earth and all its nations by
his power, for his wrath encompasses
the world and all its ways. His chariot
of victory swept over sea and mountain.
His arrows stilled the sun and moon as he
brought his salvation to his own anointed.
He crushed the wicked with his shafts of anger,
and through his whirlwind cruel men were scattered.
My body shakes, my lips are trembling at
the awesome sound. Even if crop and beast
fail to produce, I will rejoice in God,
the Lord of my salvation who is my strength.
God lifts me up to walk upon the heights.

JONAH
THE PROPHET

I

Jonah was called to go to Nineveh
to preach, but did not wish to go. He ran
away, boarding a ship sailing for Tarshish.
The ship was soon beset by storms and all
the crew were frightened and they felt that Jonah
should take the blame for disobeying God.
They cast him overboard, at which the storm
was stilled. Jonah was swallowed by a great,
gigantic fish, and there he stayed for three
days and three nights. So Jonah prayed for help
and the fish spat him out upon a beach.
God ordered Jonah yet again to go
to Nineveh, a city of great size.
At last he went and told the people that
their city would be overthrown if they

did not repent their evil. All the people,
even their king, fasted to show they wished
to mend their ways, so God did not destroy
the city. Jonah was upset by this because
he thought the city should be after all
destroyed. He sat beneath a shady plant,
thinking about the city. Then a worm
attacked the plant, and the sun beat upon
the head of Jonah, and he wished to die.
Jonah was sorry for the plant, but God
reminded him that Nineveh was worth
much more than any plant, and that its people
were worthy of compassion from the Lord.

DANIEL
PROPHET AND SAGE

I

THE BABYLONIANS transported Jews
from Judah so that they could train for service.
Daniel and his three friends[32] were in this group
and they found favour. Each was given a name,
and Daniel's name became Belteshazzar. These
four men adhered to Jewish ways and ate
according to their laws. Soon Daniel was
known as a sage and could interpret dreams.
King Nebuchadnezzar had a dream which troubled
his thoughts. Daniel alone could penetrate
the meaning of the dream. Daniel explained
that God inspired him. He told the king
that after his kingdom others would arise,
that four great kingdoms would be dominant,
that all would fall before God's kingdom. Then
the king gave Daniel honours, gifts and praise,
making him ruler over Babylon.
Daniel's three friends were also highly honoured.
But Nebuchadnezzar raised a mighty image
of gold which all were bound to worship. Daniel's

three friends did not bow down in worship, so
the king commanded they should be consigned
to death within a fiery furnace. But when
the king looked in the furnace four men walked
through scorching flames, an angel having come.
The three men were removed, were soon forgiven,
and then regained their former high respect.

II

THE KING dreamed yet again and saw a tree
reaching to heaven, but by God's word the tree
became a stump, while a rich man became
a beast in mind and action. Daniel said
the tree was Nebuchadnezzar's kingdom, while
the beastlike man was the king. But the stump
was meant to show the kingdom would survive
if the king truly believed in God. This came
about, for the king lost his mind, but later
on was restored to normal, crown in place,
because he honoured God in all his works.
Another king arose: Belshazzar was
his name. He gave a splendid feast and all
gave praise to their false gods. A hand appeared
and wrote upon the wall, and only Daniel
was able to interpret what was written.
Daniel then read as follows: *Soon your kingdom
will end, for you are weighed and found to be
wanting. So Medes and Persians will divide
your kingdom up.* That night the king was slain
and in his place Darius the Mede ruled.
Still Daniel held a high position, but
soon rivals told the king that Daniel broke
the law by worshipping his God. With great
reluctance, king Darius told his men
that Daniel must be placed inside a den
of lions. But overnight the lions did not
assault Daniel and he was taken out.
Then his accusers were devoured by

the lions, while Daniel prospered through the reigns
of king Darius and the Persian Cyrus.
The God of Daniel was then feared by all.

III

DANIEL had visions in the night. He saw
four beasts emerging from the sea, and learned
that these were signs of kingdoms yet to come,
all ruled by kings who victimized the saints
faithful to God. He saw enthroned on flames
of fire the ancient of days, Almighty Judge,
who held his court before the saints. There came
on heavenly clouds one like a son of man:
to him was given by the ancient of days,
glory, dominion and power over the earth
and all its peoples. Though the fourth supreme
kingdom would rule the world, the saints of God
would yet prevail under the power of heaven.
Daniel then saw a two horned ram at war
with a one horned goat which won victory
over the ram. The goat grew strong, but lost
its power. Another horn arose and grew
until it overthrew the sanctuary where
the offerings were made. Two angels spoke
and said that in God's time the holy place
would be restored. Gabriel said to Daniel,
Your vision is about the power of kings
who will cause great destruction in the world.
A mighty king will rise against the Prince
of princes, but his wicked power will break,
though not by human hands. Now seal this vision,
for it speaks ahead of future happenings.

IV

DANIEL well knew that Israel's sad fate had
come upon them for not abiding by

the law of Moses. So he prayed that God
in his great mercy would restore his people,
and take them back to build Jerusalem again.
Gabriel said to Daniel: *Many years*
will pass before the holy city is
restored. A holy one will come, and then
another, who will be cut down. A prince
will cause great desolation, but the end
will bring destruction for the desolator.
Daniel again had visions, and he saw
an apparition of a man who was formed
like jewels and lightning and bronze. His voice was like
the sound of many people. Daniel bowed
down to the ground and the man said, *Fear not,*
for I have heard your speaking, though the time
is not quite yet. Michael the prince will fight
along with me against the prince of Persia.
Kings shall arise and wars shall come about
in great confusion; but one king will conquer
many lands and he will make himself as god,
setting himself against the God of gods. One day,
even that king will end his rule. Then shall
arise Michael, your great prince and there will
be many troubles. The dead will leave the dust
to meet their judgement, and the righteous will
be like bright stars. A man seen in my vision
told me to keep my thoughts until the end.
Then he revealed that by the end of days
a vile abomination would usurp
the place of sacrifice in desolation.

MALACHI
THE PROPHET

I

GOD SAYS, *I have loved Israel, but my priests*
have no regard for me, their father. How
can I show favour to you when you offer
polluted sacrifices? I refuse
your offerings, for though my name is great
among the nations, you weary of service.
You will receive my curse and not my blessing
and I will thrust you from my presence, for
you have fallen from the honourable ways
of Levi, who used to walk in peace with me
and followed righteous ways. My covenant
is now corrupt, so you will brought low.
Malachi says that Judah has been faithless,
though God is father to us all. You have
married the daughter of an alien god,
and left the Lord your husband. Your God
desires godly offspring, but he is
weary of empty words, so have a care.

II

MY MESSENGER prepares my way: the Lord
whom you expect will suddenly appear.
There in the temple you will see with joy
the messenger of the Lord's covenant.
Who will be able to stand on that day?
Who will endure his pure, refining fire?
The sons of Levi will be cleansed until
their offerings are right and good. The Lord
will judge all wrongdoers. He does not change,
though all the sons of Jacob have transgressed.
If you return to him, then surely he
will turn again to you. The curse is yours
for now you steal his tithes. If you repent,

the blessing will be yours. Those who fear
the Lord will be his proud possession. They
must separate the evil from the good,
and learn to serve him well. The day is coming
when arrogant men are burned, from root to branch.
Then righteousness will be like dawn, and healing
will touch you with its wings. Remember then
the laws of Moses, for Elijah, God's
prophet will come again on that great day,
that terrifying day when the Lord comes.

NOTES

1   Jethro and Reuel are alternative names for the father-in-law of Moses.
2   Horeb and Sinai are alternative names for the holy mountain.
3   That is, the Red Sea. The Hebrew name translates as the *Reed Sea*.
4   In Hebrew, *Jerubaal*.
5   This is only part of Hannah's song quoted from I Samuel 2:1.
6   *Ichabod* means "Where is the glory".
7   The Philistines were known as the "uncircumcised".
8   In Hebrew there is a pun on the word for *summer fruit* and the word for *end*.
9   Many commentators believe that the ideas presented here (based on Amos 9:11–15) are an editorial comment, possibly written after the Babylonian Exile.
10 Here Israel refers to the northern kingdom which was overrun by the Assyrians in 721 BC.
11 In Hebrew the word for Baal has several meanings, one of which is *husband*.
12 In the poems about Isaiah of Jerusalem, Isaiah Chapters 1–39 have been used, with omissions, because some passages are thought to be of a later period.
13 In Hebrew the name means *God-with-us*.
14 In Hebrew the name means *A-remnant-shall-return*, being a prophecy of the future return of some captives.
15 In Hebrew the name means *The-spoil-speeds-the prey-hastes,* a sign of Assyria's power.
16 Chapters 40–55 of the Book of Isaiah are thought to be the work of an anonymous prophet who followed his calling during the latter part of the Babylonian Exile.
17 Zedekiah.
18 A group founded by Jehonadab several generations previously. They eschewed strong drink and lived in tents like the Israelites of old.
19 The capital of the northern kingdom of Israel.
20 The capital of the southern kingdom of Judah.
21 Ephraim here refers to the northern kingdom of Israel.
22 Gog is a mythical leader who will lead the final assault against God's people. Various theories have been formulated to try to identify him as a historical figure.
23 The following sections are based on Zechariah, Chapters 9–14. Some commentators argue that these are additions to Zechariah's work.

24 A leading city in the Persian empire.
25 A Persian city.
26 Eliphaz.
27 Bildad.
28 Zophar.
29 The place of the dead.
30 Elihu.
31 The Hebrew word used here means "faithfulness", though some versions translate as "faith". There is a measure of ambiguity in the word "his" (a suffix in Hebrew). Does "his" refer to God's faithfulness or to man's faithfulness?
32 Hananiah (= Shadrach), Mishael (= Meshach) and Azariah (= Abednego).